FAITHS &
RELIGIONS
OF THE WORLD

FAITHS & RELIGIONS
OF THE WORLD

DAVID GIBBONS

THUNDER BAY
P·R·E·S·S
San Diego, California

Thunder Bay Press
An imprint of the Advantage Publishers Group
THUNDER BAY 10350 Barnes Canyon Road, San Diego, CA 92121
P · R · E · S · S www.thunderbaybooks.com

ISBN-13: 978-1-59223-849-1
ISBN-10: 1-59223-849-1

Library of Congress Cataloging-in-Publication Data

Gibbons, David.
Faiths and religions of the world / David Gibbons.
p. cm.
Includes bibliographical references and index.
ISBN 978-1-59223-849-1 (alk. paper)
1. Religions. I. Title.
BL80.3.G53 2007
200.9--dc22

2007026608

Printed and bound in Thailand
1 2 3 4 5   11 10 09 08 07

Acknowledgments
The author and publisher wish to extend their thanks to the following
for their advice and suggestions during the preparation of this work:
Peter Bently; Dr. Kate Crosby, School of Oriental and African Studies;
Dr. Kharak Singh, Institute of Sikh Studies, Chandigarh; Sue King;
Satender Mohan; Dr. Anita Sharma, University of Delhi; Dr. Andrew
Skilton; Dr. Zafarul-Islam Khan, Director of the Institute of Islamic and
Arab Studies, New Delhi; and to Susie Green for her contributions
and support.

Publisher's note
The publisher will not assume liability for damages caused by inaccuracies
in the data and makes no warranty whatsoever expressed or implied.
Every effort has been made to ensure the accuracy of the information
presented in this book. "The Guide to Further Reading" includes
many of the books from which the information in this book has
been sourced. Every effort has been made to trace copyright holders
and seek permission to use illustrative and other material. The
Publisher wishes to apologise for any inadvertent errors or omissions
and would be glad to rectify these in future.

Designed and produced by DAG Publications Ltd., London
Maps and illustration research by Anthony A. Evans
Edited by John Gilbert

Page 1: *The Shinto "Wedded Rocks" at Futamigaura in
Ise Bay. It is believed that they sheltered Izanagi and Izanami,
the legendary creators of Japan (see page 32).*

Pages 2–3: *The pagoda of the Buddhist Yakushi temple at
Nara in Japan, built in the eighth century.*

Illustration Acknowledgments
Suzie Green: page 131 Ranakpur temple. iStockphoto: page 26 prayer; page 35 Knossos; page 33 step pyramid; page 33 Krisna; page 37
Buddhist monk statue; page 37 Philae; page 39 Paestum; page 39 vase; page 40 Teotihuacan; page 40 Sanchi; page 40 Shiva; page 42 Eight
Trigrams; page 43 Seoul temple; page 43 Ganesha; page 44 Dome of the Rock; page 44 Jokhang; page 44 Nara; page 44 Buddha statue; page
47 Cordoba; page 47 Angkor Wat; page 47 Prambanan; page 48 Toltec statues; page 48 Marrakesh; page 48 Heian shrine; page 48 Pagan; page
49 Jerusalem city walls; page 50 Jerusalem mosque; page 51 Kamakura; page 51 Gumi; page 52 Ranakpur; page 52 Mongolia; page 53 Qutub
Minar; page 53 Amiens cathedral; page 53 carved effigies; page 53 rose window; page 55 Norwich Cathedral; page 55 Buddha statue; page 55
Pura Ulun Danu; page 56 Aztec god; page 56 Reims cathedral; page 56 Golden Pavilion; page 56 Temple of Heaven; page 58 Hagia Sophia; page
58 Blue Mosque; page 59 Shwedagon Pagoda; page 61 Fountains Abbey; page 63 St. Peter's Cathedral; page 63 Toshogu shrine; page 65 St.
Paul's Cathedral; page 70 Salt Lake Temple; page 75 Christ the Redeemer; page 77 old Liverpool Cathedral; page 77 new Liverpool Cathedral;
page 78 Sagrada Familia; page 79 Krishna temple; page 79 Potala Palace; page 93 aboriginal art; page 99 Mount Sinai; page 100 Wailing Wall;
page 100 synagogue door; page 103 Mexico City cathedral; page 107 St. Petersburg; page 108 Methodist church; page 110 reading the Qur'an;
page 111 Blue Mosque; page 112 ablutions; page 112 performing *rakah*; page 115 Djenné; page 116 Sabah State Mosque; page 117 Baha'i
House of Worship; page 118 cremation; page 123 River Ganges; page 130 Shantinatha; page 130 Ranakpur; page 134 *gurdwara*; page 135
Golden Temple; page 137 Temple of Heaven; page 138 Confucius; page 140 Tin Hau temple; page 141 shrine; page 144 torii gate; page 146
Kasuga Taisha; page 146 Meiji shrine; page 147 Yasaka shrine; page 147 Hachiman shrine; page 147 Heian shrine; page 148 plaques; page 149
fox statue; page 149 Inari shrine; page 150 Yasukuni shrine; page 151 Fushima shrine. U.S. Department of Defense: page 6 Cairo; page 44
Karbala mosque; page 74 cremation ovens; page 74 concentration camp survivors; page 75 torii gate; page 77 Kaiser Wilhelm Memorial Church;
page 78 Mormon Temple; page 80 Osama Bin Laden; page 80 Samarra mosque; page 104 St. Patrick's Cathedral; page 114 Karbala; page 132
Sikh soldiers; page 154 cargo. U.S. National Archive: page 127 Dalai Lama. Werner Forman Archive: page 1 Wedded Rocks; pages 2–3 Yakushi,
Nara; page 8 St. Mark's Basilica; page 9 Stave church; page 40 Roman relief; page 57 mosaic; page 118 wall painting; page 119 Mahabalipuram;
page 120 Trimurti; page 121 Vishnu; page 148 the Naiku. Werner Forman Archive/Art Institute Chicago: page 66 Portuguese carracks. Werner
Forman Archive/Coptic Museum Cairo: page 41 wooden lintel. Werner Forman Archive/Euan Wingfield: page 97 Zoroastrian relief; page 98 Fire
Temple. Werner Forman Archive/Private Collection: page 128 tirthankara; page 129 brass icon. All other ilustrations PageantPix.

CONTENTS

Introduction   6

The Geography of Belief
Origins and Spread   10
World Religions Today   20

The World's Religions Compared   14

Founders of the Great Religions   24
Glossary   28
Guide to Further Reading   30

TIMELINE   31
4000–1000 BCE   33
1000 BCE to the Common Era   36
Beginning of the Common Era to 500   40
500–1000   44
1000–1200   48
1200–1350   52
1350–1500   56
1500–1650   60
1650–1800   64
1800–1900   68
1900–1950   72
1950–2000   76
2000 to the Present   80

RELIGIONS   81
The Religion of Ancient Egypt   82
Religion in Ancient Mesopotamia   84
Religion in Ancient Greece   86
The Religions of Ancient Rome   88
Early Religions of Northern Europe   90
Primal and Indigenous Religions   92
The Indigenous Religions of the Americas   94
Zoroastrianism   96
Judaism   98
Christianity   102
Islam   110
Bahá'i Faith   117
Hinduism   118
Buddhism   124
Jainism   128
Sikhism   132
The Religions of China   136
The Religions of Japan   144
Alternative and New Religions   152

Index   **158**

INTRODUCTION

The aim of this book is to provide a concise, easy-to-use guide to the history of the faiths and religions of the world. It may be thought that, with so many books on religion already, what need is there for a new one? This book does something different—it shows the histories of the major religions in parallel, across the pages of a chronological diagram. This enables the reader to see how each religion was faring at any given moment in time. The timeline is arranged chronologically and geographically, across some six thousand years, from the earliest civilizations to the present day. Visually seamless, it is joined by foldout charts to present an uninterrupted sequence of events; within the foldouts, specific aspects of the time period of the chart are explained and amplified.

The timeline, which begins at about 4000 BCE, when evidence points to the first identifiable civilizations appearing, is prefaced by a selection of creation myths and legends. It ends at the present day, with the events and issues of our modern world in the twenty-first century.

Preceding the timeline is a world map that shows where the great religions originated and how they spread; another map shows the faiths of the countries of the world today. These maps are on the reverse of a six-page

Right: Roof of a Hindu temple in Singapore decorated with gods and goddesses

Below: The skyline of Cairo today

AFRICA

Algeria Sunni Muslim (state religion) 99%, Christian and Jewish 1%

Angola Indigenous 47%, Roman Catholic 38%, Protestant 15% (1998 estimates)

Benin Indigenous 50%, Christian 30%, Muslim 20%

Botswana Christian 71.6%, Badimo 6%, other 1.4%, unspecified 0.4%, none 20.6% (2001 census)

Burkina Faso Muslim 50%, indigenous 40%, Christian (mainly Roman Catholic) 10%

Burundi Roman Catholic 62%, Protestant 5%, indigenous 23%, Muslim 10%

Cameroon Indigenous 40%, Christian 40%, Muslim 20%

Central African Republic Indigenous 35%, Protestant 25%, Roman Catholic 25%, Muslim 15%; animistic beliefs and practices strongly influence the Christian majority

Chad Muslim 51%, Christian 35%, animist 7%, other 7%

Congo (Zaire) Roman Catholic 50%, Protestant 20%, Kimbanguist 10%, Muslim 10%, other syncretic sects and indigenous beliefs 10%

Congo Christian 50%, animist 48%, Muslim 2%

Cote d'Ivoire (Ivory Coast) Muslim 35–40%, indigenous 25–40%, Christian 20–30% (2001); majority of foreigners (migratory workers) are Muslim (70%) and Christian (20%)

Djibouti Muslim 94%, Christian 6%

Egypt Muslim (mostly Sunni) 90%, Coptic 9%, Christian 1%

Equatorial Guinea Nominally Christian and predominantly Roman Catholic, some pagan practices

Eritrea Muslim, Coptic Christian, Roman Catholic, Protestant

Ethiopia Muslim 45–50%, Ethiopian Orthodox 35–40%, animist 12%, other 3–8%

Gabon Christian 55–75%, animist, Muslim less than 1%

Gambia Muslim 90%, Christian 9%, indigenous 1%

Ghana Christian 63%, Muslim 16%, indigenous 21%

Guinea Muslim 85%, Christian 8%, indigenous 7%

Guinea-Bissau Indigenous 50%, Muslim 45%, Christian 5%

Guyana Christian 50%, Hindu 35%, Muslim 10%, other 5%

Kenya Protestant 45%, Roman Catholic 33%, indigenous 10%, Muslim 10%, other 2%; majority of Kenyans are Christian, but estimates for the percentage of the population that adheres to Islam or indigenous beliefs vary widely

Lesotho Christian 80%, indigenous 20%

Liberia Indigenous 40%, Christian 40%, Muslim 20%

Libya Sunni Muslim 97%

Madagascar Indigenous 52%, Christian 41%, Muslim 7%

Malawi Christian 79.9%, Muslim 12.8%, other 3%, none 4.3% (1998 census)

Mali Muslim 90%, indigenous 9%, Christian 1%

Mozambique Catholic 23.8%, Muslim 17.8%, Zionist Christian 17.5%, other 17.8%, none 23.1% (1997 census)

Mauritania Muslim 100%

Morocco Muslim 98.7%, Christian 1.1%, Jewish 0.2%

Namibia Christian 80–90% (Lutheran at least 50%), indigenous 10–20%

Niger Muslim 80%, indigenous and Christian 20%

Nigeria Muslim 50%, Christian 40%, indigenous 10%

Rwanda Roman Catholic 56.5%, Protestant 26%, Adventist 11.1%, Muslim 4.6%, indigenous 0.1%, none 1.7% (2001)

Senegal Muslim 94%, Christian 5% (mostly Roman Catholic), indigenous 1%

Sierra Leone Muslim 60%, indigenous 30%, Christian 10%

Somalia Sunni Muslim

South Africa Zion Christian 11.1%, Pentecostal/Charismatic 8.2%, Catholic 7.1%, Methodist 6.8%, Dutch Reformed 6.7%, Anglican 3.8%, other Christian 36%, Muslim 1.5%, other 2.3%, unspecified 1.4%, none 15.1% (2001 census)

Sudan Sunni Muslim 70% (in north), indigenous 25%, Christian 5% (mostly in south and Khartoum)

Swaziland Zionist 40% (a blend of Christianity and indigenous ancestral worship), Roman Catholic 20%, Muslim 10%, Anglican, Bahai, Methodist, Mormon, Jewish, and other 30%

Tanzania Mainland Christian 30%, Muslim 35%, indigenous 35%; Zanzibar more than 99% Muslim

Togo Indigenous 51%, Christian 29%, Muslim 20%

Tunisia Muslim 98%, Christian 1%, Jewish and other 1%

Uganda Roman Catholic 33%, Protestant 33%, Muslim 16%, indigenous 18%

Western Sahara Muslim

Zambia Christian 50–75%, Muslim and Hindu 24–49%, indigenous 1%

Zimbabwe Syncretic (part Christian, part indigenous) 50%, Christian 25%, indigenous 24%, Muslim and other 1%

ISLANDS AND SMALLER STATES

American Samoa Christian Congregationalist 50%, Roman Catholic 20%, Protestant and other 30%

Andorra Roman Catholic

Anguilla Anglican 29%, Methodist 23.9%, other Protestant 30.2%, Roman Catholic 5.7%, other Christian 1.7%, other 5.2%, none or unspecified 4.3% (2001 census)

Antigua Christian (predominantly Anglican with other Protestant, and some Roman Catholic)

Aruba Roman Catholic 82%, Protestant 8%, Hindu, Muslim, Confucianist, Jewish

Bahamas Baptist 35.4%, Anglican 15.1%, Roman Catholic 13.5%, Pentecostal 8.1%, Church of God 4.8%, Methodist 4.2%, other Christian 15.2%, none or unspecified 2.9%, other 0.8% (2000 census)

Barbados Protestant 67% (Anglican 40%, Pentecostal 8%, Methodist 7%, other 12%), Roman Catholic 4%, none 17%, other 12%

Bermuda Anglican 23%, Roman Catholic 15%, African Methodist Episcopal 11%, other Protestant 18%, other 12%, unaffiliated 6%, unspecified 1%, none 14% (2000 census)

British Virgin Islands Protestant 86% (Methodist 33%, Anglican 17%, Church of God 9%, Seventh-Day Adventist 6%, Baptist 4%, Jehovah's Witnesses 2%, other 15%), Roman Catholic 10%, none 2%, other 2% (1991)

Cape Verde Roman Catholic (infused with indigenous beliefs); Protestant (mostly Church of the Nazarene)

Comoros Sunni Muslim 98%, Roman Catholic 2%

Cook Islands Cook Islands Christian Church 55.9%, Roman Catholic 16.8%, Seventh-Day Adventist 7.9%, Mormon 3.8%, other Protestant 5.8%, other 4.2%, unspecified 2.6%, none 3% (2001 census); majority of foreigners (migratory workers) are Muslim (70%) and Christian (20%)

Dominica Roman Catholic 77%, Protestant 15% (Methodist 5%, Pentecostal 3%, Seventh-Day Adventist 3%, Baptist 2%, other 2%), other 6%, none 2%

Dominican Republic Roman Catholic 95%

Falkland Islands Primarily Anglican, Roman Catholic, United Free Church, Evangelist Church, Jehovah's Witnesses, Lutheran, Seventh-Day Adventist

Faroe Islands Evangelical Lutheran

Fiji Christian 52% (Methodist 37%, Roman Catholic 9%), Hindu 38%, Muslim 8%, other 2%; Fijians are mainly Christian, Indians are Hindu, and there is a Muslim minority

French Polynesia Protestant 54%, Roman Catholic 30%, other 10%, none 6%

Grenada Roman Catholic 53%, Anglican 13.8%, other Protestant 33.2%

Guadeloupe Roman Catholic 95%, Hindu and pagan African 4%, Protestant 1%

Guam Roman Catholic 85%, other 15% (1999 estimates)

Haiti Roman Catholic 80%, Protestant 16% (Baptist 10%, Pentecostal 4%, Adventist 1%, other 1%), none 1%, other 3%; about half the population practices voodoo

Jamaica Protestant 61.3% (Church of God 21.2%, Seventh-Day Adventist 9%, Baptist 8.8%, Pentecostal 7.6%, Anglican 5.5%, Methodist 2.7%, United Church 2.7%, Jehovah's Witnesses 1.6%, Brethren 1.1%, Moravian 1.1%), Roman Catholic 4%, other (including some spiritual cults) 34.7%

Kiribati Roman Catholic 52%, Protestant (Congregational) 40%, some Seventh-Day Adventist, Muslim, Baha'i, Mormon, Church of God (1999)

Maldives Sunni Muslim

Malta Roman Catholic 98%

Marshall Islands Protestant 54.8%, Assembly of God 25.8%, Roman Catholic 8.4%, Bukot nan Jesus 2.8%, Mormon 2.1%, other Christian 3.6%, other 1%, none 1.5% (1999 census)

Martinique Roman Catholic 85%, Protestant 10.5%, Muslim 0.5%, Hindu 0.5%, other 3.5% (1997)

Mauritius Hindu 48%, Roman Catholic 23.6%, other Christian 8.6%, Muslim 16.6%, other 2.5%, unspecified 0.3%, none 0.4% (2000 census)

Mayotte Muslim 97%, Christian (mostly Roman Catholic)

Micronesia Roman Catholic 50%, Protestant 47%, other 3%

Montserrat Anglican, Methodist, Roman Catholic, Pentecostal, Seventh-Day Adventist, other Christian denominations

Nauru Christian (Protestant 67%, Roman Catholic 33%)

Netherlands Antilles Roman Catholic 72%, Pentecostal 4.9%, Protestant 3.5%, Seventh-Day Adventist 3.1%, Methodist 2.9%, Jehovah's Witnesses 1.7%, other Christian 4.2%, Jewish 1.3%, other or unspecified 1.2%, none 5.2% (2001 census)

New Caledonia Roman Catholic 60%, Protestant 30%, other 10%

Niue Ekalesia Niue (Niuean Church, a Protestant church closely related to the London Missionary Society) 61.1%, Mormon 8.8%, Roman Catholic 7.2%, Jehovah's Witnesses 2.4%, Seventh-Day Adventist 1.4%, other 8.4%, unspecified 8.7%, none 1.9% (2001 census)

Norfolk Island Anglican 34.9%, Roman Catholic 11.7%, Uniting Church in Australia 11.2%, Seventh-Day Adventist 2.8%, Australian Christian 2.4%, Jehovah's Witnesses 0.9%, other 2.7%, unspecified 15.3%, none 18.1% (2001 census)

Northern Mariana Islands Christian (Roman Catholic majority, although traditional beliefs and taboos may still be found)

Palau Roman Catholic 41.6%, Protestant 23.3%, Modekngei 8.8% (indigenous to Palau), Seventh-Day Adventist 5.3%, Jehovah's Witnesses 0.9%, Mormon 0.6%, other 3.1%, unspecified or none 16.4% (2000 census)

Papua New Guinea Roman Catholic 22%, Lutheran 16%, Presbyterian/Methodist/London Missionary Society 8%, Anglican 5%, Evangelical Alliance 4%, Seventh-Day Adventist 1%, other Protestant 10%, indigenous 34%

Pitcairn Islands Seventh-Day Adventist 100%

Puerto Rico Roman Catholic 85%, Protestant and other 15%

Réunion Roman Catholic 86%, Hindu, Muslim, Buddhist (1995)

Saint Helena Anglican (majority), Baptist, Seventh-Day Adventist, Roman Catholic

Saint Kitts and Nevis Anglican, other Protestant, Roman Catholic

Saint Lucia Roman Catholic 67.5%, Seventh-Day Adventist 8.5%, Pentecostal 5.7%, Anglican 2%, Evangelical 2%, other Christian 5.1%, Rastafarian 2.1%, other 1.1%, unspecified 1.5%, none 4.5% (2001 census)

Saint Pierre and Miquelon Roman Catholic 99%

Saint Vincent and the Grenadines Anglican 47%, Methodist 28%, Roman Catholic 13%, Hindu, Seventh-Day Adventist, other Protestant

Samoa Congregationalist 34.8%, Roman Catholic 19.6%, Methodist 15%, Mormon 12.7%, Assembly of God 6.6%, Seventh-Day Adventist 3.5%, other Christian 4.5%, Worship Centre 1.3%, other 1.7%, unspecified 0.1% (2001 census)

San Marino Roman Catholic

Sao Tome and Principe Catholic 70.3%, Evangelical 3.4%, New Apostolic 2%, Seventh-Day Adventist 1.8%, other 3.1%, none 19.4% (2001 census)

Seychelles Roman Catholic 82.3%, Anglican 6.4%, Seventh-Day Adventist 1.1%, other Christian 3.4%, Hindu 2.1%, Muslim 1.1%, other non-Christian 1.5%, unspecified 1.5%, none 0.6% (2002 census)

Solomon Islands Church of Melanesia 32.8%, Roman Catholic 19%, South Seas Evangelical 17%, Seventh-Day Adventist 11.2%, United Church 10.3%, Christian Fellowship Church 2.4%, other Christian 4.4%, other 2.4%, unspecified 0.3%, none 0.2% (1999 census)

Tokelau Congregational Christian Church 70%, Roman Catholic 28%, other 2%

Tonga Christian (Free Wesleyan Church claims over 30,000 adherents)

Trinidad and Tobago Roman Catholic 26%, Hindu 22.5%, Anglican 7.8%, Baptist 7.2%, Pentecostal 6.8%, other Christian 5.8%, Muslim 5.8%, Seventh-Day Adventist 4%, other 10.8%, unspecified 1.4%, none 1.9% (2000 census)

Turks and Caicos Islands Baptist 40%, Anglican 18%, Methodist 16%, Church of God 12%, other 14% (1990)

Tuvalu Church of Tuvalu (Congregationalist) 97%, Seventh-Day Adventist 1.4%, Baha'i 1%, other 0.6%

Vanuatu Presbyterian 31.4%, Anglican 13.4%, Roman Catholic 13.1%, Seventh-Day Adventist 10.8%, other Christian 13.8%, indigenous (including Jon Frum cargo cult) 5.6%, other 9.6%, none 1%, unspecified 1.3% (1999 census)

Virgin Islands Baptist 42%, Roman Catholic 34%, Episcopalian 17%, other 7%

Wallis and Futuna Roman Catholic 99%, other 1%

FOUNDERS OF THE GREAT RELIGIONS

While the beginnings of some of the world's great religious systems can be traced to the activities of specific individuals, not all can be accurately called "founders." Rather, they inspired or initiated phases of religious development. Indeed, several of the world's great faith systems did not originate with individual people—Shinto and Hinduism, for example, owe their origins to the evolution of ancient beliefs, while some, such as Laozi, are legendary (see page 140). The following individuals, however, are detailed here as having inspired the historical starting point of their specific religion, or had great significance in its development.

Abraham and Moses

THE KEY FIGURES IN EARLY JEWISH HISTORY

The Bible begins in the book of Genesis with the creation of the world, with Adam and Eve and their descendants, and the great flood, which only Noah and his family (together with the animals he had been instructed to place in an ark) survived. It is with Abraham, however, that the Jewish religion is said to begin, possibly around 1700 BCE.

The book of Genesis relates that Abraham was originally an inhabitant of Ur in Chaldaea with the name Abram, and was divinely inspired to move, first to Haran, then to Canaan, in Palestine. There he made a covenant with God: Abram would serve the Lord faithfully, and in return God would provide him with a son; indeed, his descendants would be "more numerous than the stars." God changed his name to Abraham—he would become the "Father of Many Nations."

His importance as the first man to recognize God and as the ancestor of the Hebrews is supplemented by his demonstration of faith when tested by God. Commanded to sacrifice his son Isaac, he was prepared to comply until his hand was stayed by an angel. He thus became a model of perfect submission to God, who thereby also demonstrated that he did not require human sacrifice.

Christians see Abraham as an exemplar of faith. Muslims call him Ibrahim, and he is seen as a prophet. It was he who restored the monotheistic worship at the Ka'aba in Mecca and is considered the original Muslim. He is the most important and (with Moses) the most frequently mentioned of the former prophets in the Qur'an.

Abraham, his son Isaac, and his grandson Jacob are considered the patriarchs, ancestors of the Jews; their wives, Sarah, Rebekah, Leah, and Rachel (Jacob had two wives) are the matriarchs.

The story of the Hebrews as recounted in the Bible becomes tribal early in the second millennium BCE, when they have settled in Egypt and fallen into servitude. The next phase in the history of the Jews was their exodus from Egypt, led by Moses.

The story of Moses is told in Exodus. That the Hebrews, despite their enslavement, had increased in number is suggested by the order of the pharaoh to kill all newborn Hebrew males, and from this fate Moses was saved by being hidden in a basket in the reeds of the Nile, where he was rescued by the pharaoh's daughter. When grown to manhood, he received a divine command to liberate the Hebrews from their Egyptian bondage. God sent down ten plagues upon Egypt to persuade the pharaoh to let them go, and Moses led the twelve tribes across the Red Sea into Sinai. There, on Mount Sinai, he received God's revelation, the Torah (Pentateuch), including the Ten Commandments, and acted as intermediary between God and his chosen people while they wandered for forty years in the wilderness. Essentially the founder of Israel, he did not live to enter the promised land and it was left to Joshua and others to conquer Palestine.

Moses occupies a unique position in Jewish tradition, and Maimonides named him the greatest of the prophets. In the Christian Gospels, he appears with Christ at the Transfiguration as representative of the law, while the Qur'an calls him Musa and says that he prophesied the coming of Muhammad.

Left: *Abraham leaves Ur upon God's command.*

Right: *A dramatic impression of Mount Sinai, as Moses receives the law from God while the Hebrew tribes watch in awe.*

The Buddha

THE FOUNDER OF THE BUDDHIST FAITH

Gautama Siddhartha was born in modern Nepal, the son of a prince or king. Traditionally, his dates are 563–483 BCE, but recent scholarship suggests later dates of *c.* 480–400 BCE. At birth it was prophesied that he would be either a great ruler or a wise man; his father, wanting the former, brought him up in a secluded environment within the palace walls, sheltered from the outside world and its problems. He married Princess Yasodhara, who bore him a son, Rahula.

One day he persuaded his chariot driver, Chandaka, to take him outside the walls, where he witnessed four things: an old man, a sick man, a corpse, and a wandering old holy man. Chandaka explained that the first three things were normal and happened to everyone—and for Siddhartha this was a life-changing experience.

He shaved his head and then departed to become an itinerant beggar, leading an austere life for six years and fasting to the extent that he nearly killed himself. Drawing back just in time, he realized he had gone too far and resolved on a middle path between luxury and austerity. So he took food and sat beneath a *bodhi* tree (or pipal tree, a fig, "the tree of wisdom") at Bodh Gaya (in present-day Bihar), determined not to move until he had resolved his understanding. During this time the god Mara, the embodiment of desire (equivalent, perhaps, to Satan in Christianity) tempted him and assailed him, but the Buddha resisted successfully.

Then, at the age of thirty-five, on the night of a full moon in May, he achieved his goal, entering deep meditation and attaining enlightenment with a full insight into the nature of existence. Henceforth he was known as the Buddha (the enlightened or awakened one). Following requests by the gods Brahma Sahampati and Indra, he traveled, taught, and gathered disciples.

His first sermon concerned the Four Noble Truths and was given in the Deer Park near Varanasi, India. He continued to teach the dharma, and is said to have taught 84,000 ways to enlightenment. Around him gathered a community of followers, the *Sangha*.

Heavenly portents are said to have foretold his death, which came at Kusinara, when he was eighty years old.

Left: *The birth of the Buddha*

Above: *During the sixth week after attaining enlightenment, the Buddha sat beneath the tree of Muchalinda, a naga, or serpent deity. A storm blew up and the cobra spread his hood above the Buddha to protect him.*

Jesus Christ
THE FOUNDER OF CHRISTIANITY

The religion of Christianity stems from the life, ministry, and death of Jesus Christ, born in Palestine just before the end of the reign of Herod the Great (who died in 4 BCE) in Bethlehem, not far from Jerusalem. According to scripture, his mother was a virgin.

Little is known of his childhood and early life until about 27–29 CE, when he was baptized by the wandering preacher John the Baptist, and then, according to the Gospels, spent forty days and nights in the wilderness meditating and resisting the temptations of the devil. He then set out as an itinerant preacher, mainly in the area of Galilee and northern Palestine. His ministry probably lasted no more than two or three years, and during this time he healed the sick, including lepers, carried out exorcisms, and was recorded as having performed miracles such as walking on water and feeding large crowds with seemingly inadequate resources. Crowds flocked to listen to him and to be healed, and around him he gathered an intimate group of twelve disciples who would, after his death, become the nucleus of a new sect.

He taught of the coming Kingdom of God, and his teachings brought him into frequent conflict and debate with the Jewish religious authorities. His essential differences with Judaism included seeing the ceremonial as secondary to basic principles such as as charity, humility, and sincerity. The Jewish leaders, who detected in him an authority claiming divinity, saw him as a challenge and a threat, not least in political terms. He was called—and admitted to being—the Messiah (Hebrew for "anointed one," invested by God with special powers and functions), but this also struck chords with Jewish nationalists—expectations of a deliverer and restorer of the Jewish kingdom were kindled, furthering his apparent threat to the establishment.

Jesus foresaw his own death, as a fulfillment of prophecies. Indicted by the Jewish authorities, he was executed by crucifixion about 29–33 CE by the Roman garrison of Jerusalem. According to the Gospels, on the third day his tomb was found to be empty, and the resurrected Christ showed himself to his disciples several times subsequently before being taken up to Heaven (the Ascension). Thereafter his disciples carried his message far and wide, converting Gentiles and making it more than a sect within Judaism. Subsequently, Christ's relationship with God became a subject of intense debate within the Christian Church (see pages 41 and 103).

Islam calls him Isa ibn Maryam (Jesus, son of Mary) and regards him as a prophet in the line that runs from Adam to Muhammad; Muslims deny his divinity, however, seeing him as a messenger confirming the pronouncements of earlier prophets.

Left: *Christ preaches on the hills by Lake Tiberius, Galilee.*

Muhammad
THE FOUNDER OF ISLAM

Muhammad ibn Abd Allah was born in 570 CE into the Hashemite clan of the Quraysh tribe in Mecca, in the area of the Hejaz in northwest Arabia. His parents died young—his father before Muhammad was born, and his mother when he was six—so Muhammad became the ward of his uncle, Abu Talib, leader of the Hashemite clan and a respected merchant in what was an important and prosperous trading city on busy trade routes. At the age of twelve, Muhammad is said to have visited Syria with his uncle on a trading expedition, and he evidently gained business experience and expertise. When he was twenty-five, he married a wealthy widow, Khadijah, fifteen years his senior, and she was to bear him seven children. He seemed destined for the prosperous life of an Arab trader.

It was in a cave in a hill northwest of Mecca, called Mount Hira, the Mountain of Light, that Muhammad's life changed. He had from time to time come here to meditate and to be alone; then, when he was around forty years old, he had a vision and a revelation. Possibly about the year 613, he is said to have been visited by the angel Jibril (Gabriel in Christian nomenclature), who ordered him to record the words of guidance that would be revealed to him by the creator and sustainer of all life. These revelations would later be collected to make up the Qur'an (literally, "the recitation").

When Muhammad began to spread his message from God, his teachings, based on his revelations, were not well received. The religious environment of the Hejaz at this time reflected its tribal society of villages and towns, where certain Judeo-Christian elements mixed with polytheism and female infanticide was not uncommon. Mecca was a focal point for idol-worshippers, and the local traders, custodians of the sacred place, made a good income from pilgrims visiting the *Ka'bah*. Muhammad's teaching of submission to the will of "the one just and merciful God" contradicted popular practices. The message that all would come to be judged for their deeds by the one and only God could be seen to transcend tribal groups, with their code of tribal honor, and was perceived as a threat to tribal leaders' authority.

His uncle's standing in the local community protected Muhammad for some years, but in 622 he was forced to flee to Yathrib (later known as Medina, the City of the Prophet), 200 miles to the north. By this time he had built up a group of followers, and at Yathrib he began to create the *umma*, a community based upon Islam. With the aid of his *ansar* (helpers), he built a mosque and began to set out the obligations and rights of adherents as revealed to him.

Hostility from Mecca continued, however, and resulted in a number of battles until finally, in 630, the Muslims (meaning "people who surrender to God") captured Mecca. Muhammad cleared the *Ka'bah* of idols, and gradually the inhabitants of the city began to adopt Islam. Muhammad died two years later, having established not only a religion but a state, which would grow to become a mighty power and spread a faith that today numbers more than a billion adherents.

Left: *A Muslim prays in Delhi.*

Right: The tomb of Set I, son of Ramses I, showing the solar bark. Sacred boats were used in rituals, emphasizing the central role of the Nile in the fortunes of the land, and Re, the sun god, crossed the heavens in a solar bark. The upper part of this composition represents life in the hidden land beyond this world, with the solar bark crossing the divisions of the underworld.

they neared the god's shrine, which might be hewn from a fifty-ton block of granite. Larger temples contained innumerable administrative and storage rooms.

Worship

For the Egyptians, it was not the images of the gods that were important but the rituals involved in their worship. The faithful did not approach the god directly or visit the deity's sanctuary. Only the higher priests might enter there.

Gods were seen as having the same needs as humanity, so after being awoken by ritual singing, the deity would be washed, dressed, and offered breakfast. He or she was then ready for the business of the day, pronouncing oracles or perhaps receiving visitors. The priests relayed the deity's declarations, which no doubt were in accord with their own wishes or political aspirations. After a day of toil interspersed with refreshment and offerings of incense, including myrrh and *kyphi*, the deity rested until morning.

The first chamber of large temples was usually a spacious forecourt, and it was here the public would come to worship their gods and present offerings. Statues of the pharaoh and other officials stood in the outer areas of the temple, and these intermediaries would pass on the prayers of the faithful to the deity.

Egyptians also had small shrines in their homes and made offerings to lesser household gods, who offered protection from the regular vicissitudes of life: scorpion bites, difficult childbirth, illness, unrequited love.

Right: The god Horus, with a falcon's head, and Anubis, with a jackal's head, weigh the soul of a deceased Egyptian noble. If bad outweighed good, the soul would be devoured by the "Great Eater"; if good outweighed bad, the soul would be reunited with the body to enter eternal life in the underworld. To the left, the Ibis-headed Thoth records the proceedings.

Festivals

During a normal day there were minor ceremonies within the temple: a special offering or perhaps a procession through the outer chambers. At other times, tales of the gods were enacted on the sacred lakes of larger temples.

Real festivals, however, were of a different order. Visiting Bubastis in 450 BCE, the Greek historian Herodotus described the temple of Bastet—a female cat-headed deity, protector of pregnant women and patron of music and dance— as surrounded by wide canals fed by the great Nile River, constructed of fine red granite, and encircled by elegant whispering trees.

Herodotus recounted that men and women sailed along the waters to the temple, "vast numbers in each boat." They struck castanets, played pipes, sang, and clapped their hands. When they reached Bubastis they celebrated the feast "with abundant sacrifices" and consumed "'more grape-wine" than during the whole of the rest of the

year. Contemporary Egyptians estimated that some 70,000 people attended the festivities.

Other gods moved along the rivers themselves, in sacred barks, or portable boats. Amun, for instance, would journey from his main temple at Thebes to his private "home" at Luxor, where he would stay with his consort, Mut. But the deity's image was still not visible to the thousands upon thousands who thronged the river banks, celebrating wildly. It was veiled, an invisible sacred presence, indicated only by a carvings of the god's head adorning the prow and stern of the bark.

ANIMALS

The ancient Egyptians did not distinguish between gods, people, or animals: all were classified as living beings. Animals, too, had a *ka* and a place in the afterlife. Many were holy and embodied in deities.

One way of invoking protection was to carry a magic knife engraved with sacred animal images such as the crocodile, the hippopotamus, and the all-important cat.

An early indication of the reverence with which the cat was held is shown by a coffin spell of c. 2000 BCE that mentions a great tomcat and asks, "Who is this great tomcat?" and answers, "He is the god Re himself"—Re being the preeminent solar god of the period. As animals had an afterlife, their tombs, such as those at the cat cemetery of Abydos (c. 1900 BCE), like those of humans, contained food and drink to sustain the animals during their perilous journey to the afterlife. Many animals were mummified. Cats, for instance, were embalmed with costly oils and aromatic scents, and their bodies dispatched to the cat-headed Bastet's temple, where they were buried in her sacred repositories or one of the other underground cat cemeteries constructed along the banks of the Nile. In 1889, 300,000 mummified cats were discovered at just one site, Beni Hassan.

RELIGION IN ANCIENT MESOPOTAMIA

Mesopotamia roughly covered the land we now know as Iraq. The Sumerians settled the lower, eastern area of Mesopotamia, through which flow the Tigris and Euphrates, and the area on the tip of the Persian Gulf, in around 4500 BCE. However, it was not until 3000 BCE that Sumeria blossomed and became the world's earliest known urban civilization. The beliefs and practices of the Sumerians and Akkadians, and their successors, the Babylonians (Old Empire, 2200–1750 BCE), the Neo-Babylonian Empire (625–539 BCE), and Assyrians (900–612 BCE), form a single stream of tradition, although as time passed, certain differences became apparent.

The Sumerian pantheon was made up of gods as capricious as humanity, and possessed all humanity's virtues and vices, as well as its natural appetites and needs. The most powerful gods were embodiments of natural forces and ruled supreme in different cities.

Some towns and deities
~ Uruk: Anu, ruler of heaven, and supreme deity
~ Inanna: the great earth mother, goddess of fertility, love, and war
~ Nippur: Enil, lord of the atmosphere
~ Eridu: Enki, ruler of the reserves of freshwater that spring from beneath the earth
~ Larsa: Utu, the sun god
~ Ur: Nanna, the moon god

Their temples dominated the towns and cities and, from the advent of the Old Empire of Babylonia in 2200 BCE, took the form of enormous ziggurats, or high multilayered temple towers.

Gods also represented objects, and in a society dependent upon agriculture, farming implements often had their own deities. Enil's son, Ninurta, for instance, was lord of the plow.

The Sumerians and the Babylonians believed that heaven and earth had once been joined in the form of an enormous mountain. Since their separation, priests had to act as intermediaries for those wishing to contact deities. The ziggurat-style temples built in 2200–500 BCE represented this mountain. The interior of the ziggurat was solid, with spiral stairs or paths on the exterior giving access to the small temple at the top, dedicated to a specific divinity.

The most famous of these ziggurats is the Tower of Babel, the construction of which is recorded in the book of Genesis. As it was built near Babylon, some believe it was an extension of the worship of Marduk, chief of the Babylonian gods. The ziggurat at Ur, in modern Iraq, was dedicated to the moon god. It still exists, though it is now named Tall al-Muqayyar.

As subject to fleshly needs as humanity, the Sumerian gods needed food to survive. They were forced to create irrigation canals to water their lands, to hoe, to till, and to harvest. Tiring of this toil, Enki created clay figures to do the work for them. Inanna gave them life, and humanity was born. Today humans must not only labor for their own sustenance but also for that of the gods. Naturally, the most usual public sacrificial offering was food, generally in the form of goats, cattle, birds, and sheep. The gods were given the right leg, the kidneys, and a succulent roasting joint; humans feasted on the rest. But the gods needed other items and were also proffered many things beloved of humanity, including clothes, furniture, jewels, and weapons. In reality, after being offered to the deities, these items were assigned to the temple treasuries.

Enki and Inanna drank to celebrate their wondrous creation but ended up quarreling. Inanna spitefully declared she could destroy what they had made and

Above: *The Hittite King Suppiluliamus II depicted as a god*

created cripples and other disabled beings. Enki, however, found a place on earth for all these unfortunates, which explains why deformity exists in the world.

Gilgamesh was the king of Uruk around 2600 BCE. A man with great personal charisma, he became the subject not only of Sumerian legend but of Hittite, Babylonian (Akkadian), and Assyrian as well. His epic reveals the futility of both fighting and the quest for immortality. Gilgamesh and his friend Enkidu go on many adventures but finally, having incurred the wrath of the gods, Enkidu's life is curtailed by disease. Gilgamesh wants to avoid this fate and determines to visit humanity's sole immortals, Utnapishtim and his wife. To show himself worthy, Utnapishtim tells Gilgamesh that he must first vanquish the lesser death, sleep, by staying awake for six days and seven nights. He fails and Utnapishtim banishes him. His wife begs mercy for the king, and so reluctantly he tells Gilgamesh of a plant growing on the ocean bed that will make him young again. Gilgamesh finds the plant but, not trusting Utnapishtim, tests its efficacy on an old man of Uruk before taking it himself. En route to Uruk, Gilgamesh stops to bathe in a lake, leaving the plant on its bank. It is eaten by a snake, who sloughs its skin and is reborn. Defeated in his quest, realizing

Above: *Marduk, the great god of the Babylonians*

VESTA

Vesta is the virgin goddess of hearth, home, and family. She is represented by a sacred flame, tended by her priestesses, the Vestal Virgins, whose duty it was to make sure it never went out. Drawn from the patricians (upper classes), the Vestal Virgins were obliged to be celibate for thirty years on pain of being buried alive in the Campus Sceleris, or Field of Wickedness. One virgin, Rhea Silvia, was raped by the god Mars, but loss of chastity by a divine force did not—at least according to some accounts of Rome's foundation myth—save her from this grisly fate.

Vesta was celebrated from June 7 to June 15, during which, for one day only, women were able to offer her sacrifices. Vesta was of great significance to women because the hearth was where the family's food was prepared. Meals were usually eaten next to it, and offerings thrown into the flames. Patterns in the fire revealed omens of the future.

Vesta's temple in Rome kept her sacred fire burning continually until toward the end of the fourth century, when Theodosius, who made Christianity the official state religion, banned it.

Hadrian's Wall in northern England. Brutal initiation rites, as indicated by archaeological finds, included branding and burying alive; these rites bonded the soldiers to one another and to the great deity whom they called Sol Invictus, or Unconquered Sun. Myth had it that Mithras was born from a rock, and in acknowledgment of this, devotees worshipped him in purpose-built cavelike structures, or Mithraea. Some fifty of these still exist in Rome today.

Cult of the Celebrity

The Greeks had already deified Alexander the Great on his death, and throughout their empire it was commonplace for absolute rulers to declare themselves divine. In Rome, however, the republican constitution meant, at least in theory, that emperors were not all-powerful dictators. This constitutional barrier to deification was set aside in 44 BCE when the senate decreed that the assassinated Julius Caesar should join the gods. As the empire became more powerful, the emperors became more autocratic and they became

what we might term celebrities, and attracted huge cult followings.

In 27 BCE, Octavian, Caesar's great-nephew, finally fought off his competitors and became emperor, styling himself as Augustus (Splendid). In Oriental and Egyptian provinces, he was seen and worshipped as a living god. Presumably, Romans also envisaged him in this light; oaths of allegiance taken by Romans trading in the provinces referred to him as "a son of god."

Henceforth, with few exceptions, emperors were automatically declared divine. Some even bestowed divinity on those they adored, as when the emperor Hadrian (117–38 CE) deified his lover Antinous, who had drowned in Egypt.

As the Roman Empire began to show signs of disintegration, the position of emperor, divine or not, became less secure, and these earthly deities began to ally themselves with a heavenly divinity to stabilize their own positions and to help unify the empire. Aurelian, for instance, who restored much discipline in an unruly army, chose Sol Invictus (Mithras) and in

274 CE inaugurated a new temple to the deity on Rome's eastern Campus Martius.

Alongside religion, philosophy in the form of Neo-Platonism—as expounded in particular by Plotinus (205–69 CE) and his successors—was also, at least for intellectuals, a thriving discipline. Steeped in knowledge of Eastern belief systems, Plotinus' cosmic view was surmounted by the One—the supreme being—from which emanated successively the Intellect and the Soul, and from which the human soul descends to the material world. Through "intellectual, ethical, and mystical endeavor" the human soul may return to the One and experience ecstatic union. Plotinus' reputed dying words, "I am trying to bring back the divine in me to the divine in all," nicely encapsulate his philosophy.

The Romans were a people who allowed a rich religious and spiritual diversity to flourish. And within this extraordinary mosaic, the Jewish faith and Christianity were, as time went by, also included. Christians, however, were convinced that the beliefs and myths of other faiths were deceptions and that only they knew the truth. Most likely because Christianity was a centralized religion and was thus thought to be a greater unifying force than other beliefs, in 381 CE it was declared the Roman state religion. The diversity of pantheism was gradually obliterated, and monotheism took center stage.

Left: *The Temple of Apollo, built around 450 BCE at Paestum*

EARLY RELIGIONS OF NORTHERN EUROPE

Northwest Europe in the Late Pre-Roman Iron Age

Until the 1960s, the term "Celtic" was applied to pre-Roman peoples who lived north of the Alps and south of the Elbe River, whose languages were thought to be similar. However, many academics now take the view that "Celtic" was simply a term used by the ancient Greeks for the barbarians who lived in these areas, and that in reality there was no generic northwestern European language, culture, art, or religion. For example, 375 different deities have been discovered in the area we now think of as France, and only seventy of them occur more than once. Nevertheless, the persistent belief that there was a cohesive ancient Celtic culture, over the centuries, created its own reality from which has sprung inspirational Celtic art, literature, myth, and self-image.

Because these early peoples did not crystallize their beliefs by writing them down, what little we know about them comes from Greek and Roman commentators, many of whom doubtless had their own agendas when reporting.

What does seem certain, however, is that like almost all early societies (see shamanism, page 33), these peoples recognized spirit and divinity in forces of nature, and in the streams, groves, or hills that were their lands. They also created statues of horses, bulls, bears, and other animals, but whether these were seen as deities in their own right or represented elemental forces of nature, we cannot know. Until they made contact with Mediterranean culture, these northwestern Europeans, with one known exception—the horned or antlered god Cernunnos—did not have anthropomorphic deities. Brennus, the leader of the Gauls who invaded Greece in 278 BCE, mocked the Greeks for having gods in human form.

Later anthropomorphic gods, however, were often linked with one particular animal; for example, Artio and bears, Epona and horses. Animals were also sacrificed, in particular horses and dogs, the creatures most important to man. Human sacrifice was also practiced. Lucan, an epic Roman poet writing in the first century, reported that three Gaulish gods demanded human sacrifice: Teutates by drowning, Esus by wounding, and Taranis by burning. Druids were reported to confine victims in large wicker cages and burn them to death.

Gods of northwestern Europe were equated to Roman gods by classical writers, which helps convey some small idea of their meaning. Thus Rosmerta, the great provider and trader, was paired with Mercury; and Ogmios, god of strength, with Hercules. But Epona, goddess of horses, horse breeding, and possibly land fertility, conquered the Roman gods and was adopted by Roman cavalrymen; her festival, alone among non-Roman gods, was celebrated in Rome.

Celtic Religions in Ireland, Gaul, and Britain

These are the areas that most closely reflect what is commonly thought of as the Celtic religion, and it is here that the Druids (which means "men of the oak tree") held sway. They were responsible for conducting religious rites. Lucan wrote, "They worship the gods in the woods without using temples." And according to Caesar, they gave rulings on religious questions and acted as judges in personal and intertribal matters of dispute.

The Druids also presided over a large variety of sacrificial rites. A twelfth-century Ulster record describes a horse sacrifice in which the king mated with a fine white mare. She was then killed and made into a soup, which the king was to drink and bathe in.

Religious festivals were based on astronomical and seasonal cycles, and the Druids were responsible for the calendar. Only one such, found in Coligny, France, is extant. Lunar and solar, and divided into sixty-two lunar months, it also shows the main Gallic religious festivals as well as auspicious and nonauspicious days.

Druid festivals include:

~ Solar cycles: spring and fall equinoxes, summer and winter solstices

STONEHENGE

Stonehenge is one of the world's most important archaeological sites, and debate still rages as to whether it was principally a scientific/astronomical site or a ceremonial one. For many years it was believed that the heel stone was a marker for midsummer sunrise; but the recent discovery of a neighbor to the heel stone has inclined many to the view that the two stones together formed a solar corridor, which framed the sunrise.

Contemporary Druids and Celts have claimed the stones as their own, whereas others argue that the henge was built prior to the Druid priesthood's existence, in three phases between 3000 and 1600 BCE. However, although the historical origins of the Druids are obscure, future archaeological investigations and theories may alter this view.

Twenty thousand individuals celebrated the summer solstice with the Druids at Stonehenge in 2005. Scientists, meanwhile, are collecting evidence that in fact it was the winter solstice, not the summer solstice, that was celebrated here.

CENTRAL AND SOUTH AMERICA

Two of the largest and earliest urban classical religions of Central and South America are lost to us. The Toltec Empire (Mexico) and the Tiahuanaco Empire (central Andes) collapsed without written record in the tenth century. The third empire, the Mayan, which dominated the lowland peninsula of the Yucatan highlands, Guatemala, and Belize, was already disintegrating.

However, these empires left us with extraordinary archaeological ruins. Mayan hieroglyphic script has recently been deciphered and the peoples who still speak Mayan languages retain something of the culture of this once-powerful society.

The Maya

For the Maya, time was considered sacred. They were advanced both astronomically and mathematically, and developed two interlinking calendars. The first, a repeating 260-day cycle, the Tzolkin, was divinatory. It consisted of thirteen numbers linked to twenty-day names of divine forces, such as the Pahuatuns (the wind deities), the four jaguar Balams that protected agriculture, or Exchel, the moon. The second calendar, important in rituals, consisted of eighteen months of twenty days each, and an unfavorable five-day month, Uayeb. Every fifty-two years an identically named day occurred, and a new cycle was begun.

Cosmologically, seven layers, ruled by thirteen heavenly deities, stretched above the earth; and the underworld, Xibalba, realm of the dead and purveyor of illness, stretched for four layers below. Every night the sun, in the form of a powerful jaguar, would traverse this unpleasant region before rising again in the east.

Blood sacrifice, as in other religions, was seen as a way to contact deities directly. Often this entailed the supplicant's own blood, shed by pulling a cord through the nose or penis, a process that induced visions. Children, prisoners, parrots, and other animals were also sacrificed.

Aztecs

The Aztecs replaced the Toltecs, and until the Spanish arrived, they dominated Central America. Their wealth, based on the cultivation of maize, allowed them to create a truly beautiful and marvelous capital, Tenochtitlán, with hanging gardens and pyramidal temples, where slaves and women were educated and priests and priestesses divided into thirty classes.

But behind this great wealth and sophistication lay terrible cosmic fear. The Aztecs believed that there were five major periods, all of which ended in calamity.

Left: A Mayan temple at Tikal, Guatemala. Begun in 600 BCE, Tikal was a major city for 1,500 years—the ruins include more than 3,000 structures.

They were then in the last period, that of the Fifth Sun, which rose in the east, though initially not appearing above the horizon. The cosmos were unstable, always capable of disintegration. In order for the fifth cycle to begin, the gods were forced to sacrifice themselves; and to continue rising, the sun demanded sacrifice in the form of human blood. The burden of providing this lay with the emperor, who was also the Aztecs' supreme priest. The solution was continuous expansionist warfare, which supplied a never-ending stream of human fodder.

Enormous, elaborate, and dramatic ceremonies, attended by thousands and lasting for days, were the setting for sacrifices. Festival processions displayed the victims—who sometimes numbered in the thousands—dressed as deities (*ixipitla*), perhaps in sympathetic memory of the gods who had already sacrificed themselves.

At the top of stepped pyramids, the chests of live prisoners were cut open with an obsidian knife and their bloody, beating hearts offered up. Their flayed skin constituted the costumes of male dancers, while their bodies were hurled down, their flesh cooked, and their skulls set on racks. Sometimes, though, their bodies were used for another purpose. Ritual fires, which must never go out, were renewed at the end of every fifty-two-year calendar cycle, and it was in the pit left by the sacrificial victim's heart that this new fire was lit.

For the Aztecs, the universe was filled with countless supernatural beings. Among them was Ometeotl, the Ultimate Being, who held within himself the fusion of all opposites; Xiuhtecuhtli, the fire god; and, crucially, Quetzalcoatl, the feathered snake, re-creator of the world, who invented agriculture and the arts.

The Incas

The mountain Incas first reached the Cuzco valley in 1200. By 1400, from their great urban capital Cuzco ("navel," or center of the earth) they dominated all the valley peoples. We know very little of these earlier cultures, but it seems that the Inca religion absorbed many of their beliefs.

Viracocha was their supreme god, the creator of all, but it was the deities who ascended from Lake Titicaca—sun, moon, and stars, and in particular those of the Milky Way—to whom they accorded maximum ritual and worship. Placed at the center of the Inca Empire was the magnificent gold-plated Temple of the Sun (although also worshipped there were the god of thunder, the moon goddess, and the star deities) from whom, like the rays of the sun, radiated forty-one invisible lines.

Along these lines lay 428 sacred *huacas* (formations), such as rocks, caves, and streams, the deities of which took on the form of animals or birds. These shrines are animate, most still exist, and people worship at them still.

As the sun was the center of the cosmos, the Inca emperor was central to his empire. On him, during this cosmic cycle, fell the burden of providing prosperity and harmony for his subjects, making him divine, a son of the sun god made flesh.

Great ritual ceremonies took place at the temple, which often lasted for days. The Incas drank great quantities of *chicha*, a beer made from maize, and danced and prayed. Llamas, who had two constellations in the Milky Way named after them, were sacrificed to the sun, sometimes in large numbers. This reflected their vital importance to the Incas. They were the empire's main means of transport through a mountainous landscape and were able to carry heavy loads. Their dung provided fuel and fertilizer, their hides leather and their flesh food.

More philosophically, the Incas were concerned with the resolution of opposites, for while everything was in conflict it might also be in harmony. On earth, they mirrored a cosmic preoccupation with opposites such as the sun and moon, male and female, by dividing their villages in two, and maintained this cosmic resolution through ritual.

ZOROASTRIANISM

Pre-Zarathustra

Zoroastrianism springs from the religion of the Indo-Iranians who settled in India and Persia between 2000 and 1500 BCE. It was into this world that the prophet Zarathustra, more commonly known in the West as Zoroaster, was born. The divine message was revealed to him through a series of visions when he was almost thirty years old.

Scriptures

Zoroastrianism was a purely oral tradition for almost 1,500 years. The *Avesta*, a collection of holy texts, was finally recorded around 400–500 CE. It was written in Avestan, a language of which no other examples have ever been found.

The "Old Avestan" texts are the words of Zarathustra himself, and consist of the *Gathas*, seventeen hymns; the *Yasna Haptanhaiti*, a short rite that accompanies daily priestly worship; and two sacred mantras.

The "Young Avestan" texts are the composite works of generations of priests and were originally twenty-one volumes recorded by hand in Iran during the Sassanid dynasty (224–642). These were all destroyed during various wars and the oldest manuscript now in existence is dated to 1323.

Because only priests could understand the *Avesta*, in the ninth and tenth centuries the Persian Zoroastrians wrote many texts in their own language, Pahlavi, both to encourage and explain Zoroastrianism, and to defend the faith against Muslim, Hindu, and Christian incursion.

Gods

The old god Ahura Mazda (Ohrmazd in Pahlavi) is the divine source of all that is good and dwells above in light.

His counterpart—like Ahura Mazda a primal creation—is Angra Mainu (Ahriman in Pahlavi), the source of evil, who dwells below in the abyss.

Ahura Mazda, with the assistance of his holy spirit, Spenta Mainyu, and six other Holy Immortals, made the heavens and the material world as a battlefield in which he and Angra Mainu were destined to fight.

Since Ahura Mazda can only create good, Zoroastrianism teaches that the material world is a perfect and tangible expression of spiritual and divine creation. Evil is chaos, violence, lying, cheating, and the urge to destroy, and it is with these things that Angra Mainu afflicted the world when he saw the Good Creation of God.

The original creation was wholly defiled: fire gave rise to smoke, Bull and First Man suffered and died. But as they lay dying, they ejaculated sperm; that of Bull grew into cattle, and First Man's gave rise to a plant whose leaves divided and created the first human couple.

Angra Mainu, seeing this miracle, attempted to leave the material world but found himself trapped; thus the battle between Ahura Mazda and Angra Mainu began and continues to this day. For the 3,000 years before Zarathustra these forces were evenly balanced; during the next 3,000 years, Angra Mainu will try desperately to destroy all that is good, but two saviors, created from the seed of Zarathustra, appear at thousand-year intervals, and each of them destroys part of the evil Angra Mainu has created.

During this time humanity also plays its part in reducing or increasing evil. Individuals, possessing free will, are responsible for their own fate and can choose to augment the good in the world by behaving ethically and rejecting the chaos of evil, including the demons of deceit and destruction.

When Zoroastrians die, it is their spirit, not their physical form, which is judged on the dawn of the fourth morning. If their good deeds, thoughts, and words outweigh the bad, they are accepted in heaven; if not, they must descend to hell until the time of the final resurrection and judgment. In hell, punishment is not pain for its own sake, but is inflicted to bring understanding, correction, and redemption. Therefore, those in hell experience how they behaved in the world toward others; a man who beat his wife might in turn be beaten by someone he loves and be powerless to defend himself.

The last judgment will be led by a third savior, Saoshyant, who will bodily raise the dead. After the judgment, humans will return briefly to heaven or hell, to be rewarded or corrected in their bodily form before they pass through a river of molten metal and finally emerge to live in the perfection of

Above: *A relief detail of Ahura Mazda at Persepolis, Iran, dated to the first half of the fifth century BCE.*

good for eternity with Ahura Mazda. In Zoroastrianism, body and soul, the material and the spiritual, must be in harmonious balance and are of equal importance. This is why the dead are judged once in spirit when they die and again in their bodies at the last judgment.

The molten metal will level the earth, removing the valleys and mountains that an angry Angra Mainu made when he shook the earth long ago, and finally it will fill his domain, the abyss. Evil will be extinguished for all time. At last, Ahura Mazda will reign supreme.

This will not be a catastrophic end to the earth, terminating Ahura Mazda's Good Creation. Instead, this will be the moment when heaven and earth combine; it will be the perfection of everything.

The material earth, created by Ahura Mazda, is good, and so it is not to be rejected, or abused. There is no original sin; humanity is not born to atone but to enjoy the world's bounty without destruction. Fasting, asceticism, celibacy,

AHURA MAZDA'S SEVEN CREATIONS		
Holy Immortal	*Creation*	*Quality*
Kshhathra Vairya	Sky	Desirable dominion, power
Haurvatat	Waters	Health, wholeness
Spenta Armaiti	Earth	Piety
Ameretat	Plants	Long life
Vohu Manah	Animals	Good intent
Spenta Mainu	Man	Holy spirit
Asha Vahishta	Fire	Truth, righteousness, order

and the monastic life—all avoid the earth's goodness, while gluttony and philandering abuse it.

Inherent in this is the duty to care for, be aware of, and be responsible for Ahuru Mazda's seven creations. Each is protected and inhabited by one of the seven Holy Immortals who helped Ahuru Mazda create the world. These beings are aspects of the Good Lord and so may be worshipped as individual deities. They also represent qualities that Zoroastrians should embrace and make part of themselves.

Caring for the seven creations makes Zoroastrianism an ecological faith. Although the earth's bounty may be increased by cultivation and animal husbandry, wanton destruction of nature, desecration, and pollution defile the earth and the seven creations.

A further duty is to obtain wealth and prosperity honestly and without causing harm to other human beings. Coupled with a duty to spread good in the world, this leads to large-scale compassionate philanthropy. Zoroastrian communities have substantial welfare organizations that provide subsidized housing, as well as money for education and medical care, and for those in need.

Zarasthustra proclaimed that "misery drives away the divine," and so Zoroastrians strive to spread joy through the world and be happy within themselves.

Right thoughts, deeds, and words ultimately lead to happiness: in this sense, choosing the good qualities beloved of Ahura Mazda and caring for his creations is happiness, while choosing those of Angra Mainu brings misery. This is at the heart of Zarathustra's visionary revelations.

Worship: The Fire Temple

Righteousness is represented by fire, and living flame is the sacred focus of Zoroastrian temples, which are comprised of a large, completely plain prayer room attached to a fire sanctuary. A door allows the priest to enter and exit, and windows permit the faithful to observe the ever-burning sacred fire within. Set outside the door is a ladle containing the fire's residue of ash.

There are no set rituals and no specific times to worship. Individuals simply bow, touching the ground with their foreheads, leave an offering of wood to feed the fire, and take a pinch of the sacred ash. They then pray privately. Temple prayer is not obligatory, but it is necessary to pray in the presence of ritually clean fire, even a hearth fire at home.

Men and women have equal access to the temple and the priests perform ceremonies on their behalf.

Above: *The fire temple at Isfahan, Iran. Such temples were the most important places of worship for Zoroastrians, the sacred fire buring inside symbolizing the battle against evil.*

Purity

Intrinsic to good is purity, cleanliness, and tidiness; dirt and disorder are a manifestation of chaos and thus of Angra Mainu. Orthodox Zoroastrians do not, for instance, drink from unwashed glasses or take baths, which involves wallowing in one's own dirt. Menstruation, or conditions such as suppurating boils or wounds, compromise bodily purity. Thus the orthodox Zoroastrians do not attend the Fire Temple or even touch a prayer book.

Ceremonies and Rites of Passage

Childhood initiation into Zoroastrianism is known as *navjote*. When children reach seven to nine years of age, boys and girls are each given a sacred white cotton vest (*sudreh*) and a sacred woven lamb's wool cord (*kusti*), which wraps three times around their waist. Zarathustra chose these items to remind the wearer of their duty to fight evil, to promote truth, and reject lying. They are worn for life and bestow identity and give some spiritual protection.

Marriage

This is a joyous union in accord with Good Creation and unites the couple in the spiritual and material world. Zarathustra said: "Marriage should be based on Truth, as it shall be of good gain to each."

Zoroastrians marry others who are born to the faith, as it is not deemed acceptable, or perhaps even possible, to convert others, and those not of the faith are ritually impure.

This has led to a static, now-declining number of Zoroastrians. The largest community is in Mumbai, and numbers under 100,000.

Death

Death is the temporary triumph of Angra Mainu; and dead matter, because it putrifies, is a polluting agent. Disposal of dead bodies is a matter of ritual carried out by designated corpse-bearers. After immersion in bull's urine and other rites, the naked body is exposed to the elements in a roofless circular stone tower known as a *dakhma*, or "tower of silence." Vultures devour the flesh, while the bones are purified and dried by the sun. The remains are removed to a pit lined with lime and black salt, where the action of these agents reduces them to dust.

The deceased's relatives are responsible for comforting the soul in its new environment, and so for the first year monthly ceremonies are held, as well as ten days of rituals before the Zoroastrian year's end. The ceremonies are continued yearly for the duration of one generation, about twenty to thirty years.

Holy Days

Zarathrustra named seven obligatory holy days. Of these, the most important is the No Ruz, or new year festival. No Ruz honors Ahura Mazda and the creation of fire, and looks forward to the ultimate triumph of good. This is celebrated with communal feasting, religious ceremonies, and presents.

The other six holy days celebrate the other six creations of Ahura Mazda and are known as *gahambars*; these tend to be celebrated only by Zoroastrians living in Iran.

Zoroastrians also make pilgrimages—in Iran, to ancient sacred sites in the mountains; and in India, to the oldest sacred fire, which is at Udwada.

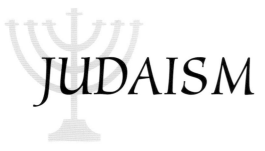

JUDAISM

Judaism has its origins in the ancient world of Abraham, Isaac, and Jacob, of Egypt, Babylon, and the promised land. For most religious Jews, the past is not simply history—it is something that has been woven into the way that they live today.

SCRIPTURES

Although the Jewish faith has a rich oral tradition, which is believed to go back to the time of Moses, it is the sacred texts that are crucial to belief and ritual. This is exemplified by a first-century legend that tells of a Roman soldier who defaced a copy of the Torah. The rage of the Jews was so fierce that, fearing insurrection, the Roman authorities were forced to execute him.

The Torah

The Torah, or the Law, is comprised of the divine teachings revealed by God to the prophet Moses on Mount Sinai and were given directly by God. In essence, the Torah is the Pentateuch, or the first five books of the Old Testament: Genesis, Exodus, Leviticus, Numbers, and Deuteronomy. The Torah can also have a wider meaning. It contains oral rabbinical ethical teachings, as these too were given to Moses by God, and have been passed down from generation to generation since that time. Thus it may be said to include all Hebrew scriptures, for they too are divinely inspired.

According to tradition, the One God revealed 613 commandments to Moses; these divide into two strands—those concerned with rituals and obligations between God and man, and judgments, rituals, and moral laws, which society would naturally have come to adopt, even without God's revelations.

Tanakh

This defines Hebrew scripture in its entirety. It falls into three sections.
1. The Torah, or the Pentateuch.
2. The *Nevi'im*, or the Prophets. These books contain the history of the Jews from their arrival in Israel to their exile in Babylon, as well as religious and moral visions. The revelations contained in these books were delivered by prophecy, not by God speaking directly to the prophets as he did when addressing Moses.

Books of the major prophets are: Joshua, Judges, Samuel (I, II), Kings (I, II), Isaiah, Jeremiah, and Ezekiel.

Books of the minor prophets are: Hosea, Joel, Amos, Obadiah, Jonah, Micah, Nahum, Habukkuk, Zephaniah, Haggai, Zechariah, and Malachai.
3. The *Ketuvim*, or Writings, also known as the *Hagiographa*. These books were conveyed by the Holy Spirit. They contain wisdom, literature, poetry, and history; some books are seen as liturgy, or ritual. These are: Psalms, Proverbs, Job, Song of Songs, Ruth, Lamentations, Ecclesiastes, Esther, Daniel, Ezra-Nehemiah, and Chronicles (I, II).

Mishna

These are the oral teachings of the Torah, written down about 200 CE. As such, they form an unbroken tradition going back to Moses. The Mishna contains the *halkakhot*, or the rules that govern Jewish daily life, including civil and criminal law, the relationship between men

Left: A highly decorated Torah

and women, and ritual purity. It—and its later explanatory companion—are used as references for decision making.

Talmud

This work of four million words enshrines the thoughts, attitudes, and opinions of hundreds of rabbis gathered through seventeen generations, from the first to fifth centuries. Its contents are extraordinarily varied. Along with commentary on the Torah and Mishna, it includes (according to Hyam Maccaby's anthology of the Talmud) passages on subjects such as enjoying nature, against asceticism, physical beauty, arguing for pleasure, and eating and drinking. This is not so much a book of rabbinical answers, as of questions. It is man in curious discourse with God.

Judaism is an absolute monotheistic religion, accepting the existence of no other gods. For Jews, the One God created heaven and earth according to Genesis, and his prophet was Moses. Judaism believes that God chose to reveal to them—over all the nations on earth—the Torah.

THE ESSENCE OF JUDAISM

Intrinsic to this conviction of being the chosen people is the belief that this One God, who redeemed them from suffering in Egypt—or an anointed one of God, a descendant of the line of David—will finally gather all Jews to the promised land, the land of Israel, and that this will herald the beginning of the messianic age.

Judaism has always believed that the precepts of its faith are continuous from the time of Moses. And although there is acceptance that religion does change over time, for religious Jews it is a crucial part of their faith that the principles of interpretation are unchanging.

In the twelfth century, Jewish intellectuals attempted to reconcile their religion with the then-preeminent philosophy of Aristotle. Foremost among these was the Sephardic rabbi Moses ben Maimon (1135–1204), known in English as Maimonides, who wrote the enormously influential work *Guide for the Perplexed*. In essence, this identified thirteen principles of the Jewish faith (see box, oppsite page).

Maimonides and his fellow Jewish philosophers were principally concerned with universal truths. The conviction held by so many that the Jews alone were the chosen people was not, to them, seen as important. Although Maimonides' thirteen principles have, for differing reasons, been criticized by subsequent scholars, over time they have become more or less the accepted creed of Judaism.

Art and Incorporeality

As Judaism stresses the incorporeality of God, its followers have always sought to avoid the idolatry they saw in Christian art. As early as the first century, rabbis forbade any naturalistic or figurative art in deference to Exodus 20:4–5, which forbade the making of graven images.

Since the visual arts—except for the making of ritual items and the embellishment of manuscripts—were not available as a means of creativity, the Jews developed rich oral traditions in poetry, music, and literature, folklore, and mystical inquiry. These are the art forms that in contemporary times also embrace theater, the novel, and the cinema, and remain the Jewish people's preeminent forms of cultural expression.

Orthodox and Ultraorthodox Judaism

Orthodoxy is Judaism's most traditional and crystallized form, in which all of life is governed by the Law and the Torah. It considers itself to be the only true Jewish religion.

During the first half of the nineteenth century, Orthodox Judaism became an organized movement in an attempt to keep at bay the blossoming Reform movement (see page 101), which sought to modernize and liberalize Judaism. Today some Orthodox Jews—though not the Ultraorthodox—may also attend more liberal synagogues.

Other, more liberal forms of Judaism observe the following festivals and rituals to varying extents and have reinterpreted Judaism to differing degrees.

Left: *Mount Sinai, where Moses received the written and oral laws from God, including the Ten Commandments*

JEWISH FESTIVALS AND HOLY DAYS

~ **New Year**: Rosh Hashanah (1–2 Tishrei). Thirty days before Rosh Hashanah, Jews begin forty days of penitence. At Rosh Hashanah a ram's horn (*shofar*) is blown in the synagogue as a call to remind the Jews of their shortcomings, and God, in divine judgment, determines the fate of the coming year. Jews eat sweet foods and those that symbolize sweetness in recognition of the bounty of God and their confidence in his mercy. Bread is dipped in honey instead of the usual salt.

~ **Day of Atonement**: Yom Kippur (10 Tishrei). This marks the end of the forty days of penitence and is the Jewish year's most sacred and solemn day. At its heart is *teshuva*—return to God—and a commitment to behave correctly during the next year. Synagogues are full on this day as Jews ask God for forgiveness. Intrinsic in this, however, is that Jews must first have sought forgiveness from those they have sinned against.

Yom Kippur is marked by a strict twenty-five-hour fast—dawn till dusk the following day. Other prohibitions apply to work, sex, washing (except strictly for hygiene), wearing leather shoes (they symbolize comfort), and being anointed with oils.

~ **Tabernacles**: Succot (begins on 15–16 Tishrei). This festival commemorates the time the Israelites spent wandering in the wilderness after the Exodus from Egypt. Its most important ritual involves holding together branches of palm, willow, myrtle, and an etrog, a type of citrus fruit, while praying. The last day of the festival is the Time of Rejoicing, which is celebrated in the synagogue with dancing, singing, and drinking.

~ **Hannukkah** (25–30 Kislev). This is an eight-day festival of lights that celebrates the victory of Judas Maccabaeus and his Jewish followers over the Syrian rulers of Palestine in the second century. During this festival an eight-branched candelabra, known as a menorah, has one more candle lit each night, to celebrate the "miracle of the oil": when the Maccabees (Hasmoneans) reclaimed their temple they had only enough oil to keep the menorah burning for one night—but miraculously, it burned for eight.

~ ***Purim*** (14 Adar). This commemorates the events of the book of Esther in which the Jews of the Persian Empire were saved

Left: At the Wailing Wall in Jerusalem

from the murderous machinations of Haman. This is a joyous festival with presents and much eating and drinking—even drinking to excess, until you are unable to distinguish between the good deeds of Mordecai, the hero of this history, and the evil actions of Haman, is desirable because it demonstrates symbolically that the form taken by God's help may be beyond what humanity is able to understand or discern.

~ **Passover**: Pesach (15–16 Nisan). This seven-day festival celebrates the Exodus, when the Jews left Egypt. No leavened bread may be eaten during this time. This is because when the Jews left Egypt in a hurry, the only bread they could take with them was unleavened. The form it takes today is matzo, a thin wafer of unleavened bread.

On the first night two nights a symbolic meal, the *Seder*, is eaten. This comprises three pieces of matzo; *maror* (bitter herbs), which represent the bitter time of slavery in Egypt; a bowl of salt water, which represents the tears that were shed (eaten by dipping parsley in it); and *haroset*, a sweet paste of almonds, apples, and wine, the consistency of which reminds Jews of the mortar they used when being forced to build in Egypt but which also denotes the sweetness of deliverance. The ceremonial plate also has on it a roasted egg that stands for the offerings taken to the Temple for the festival. Four glasses of wine are drunk, to represent the four stages of redemption the will culminate in the Messiah's coming.

Sabbath: *Shabbat*

This weekly festival commemorates both the creation of the world and the Israelites' deliverance from Egypt. It is celebrated mainly in the home, the traditional center of Jewish life. It starts at sunset on Friday, when the Shabbat candles are blessed and lit by the mother of the family, and ends at sunset on Saturday. The father, along with with his children, often visits the synagogue on Friday evening, and when he returns home he blesses his wife before the family sits down to eat.

Shabbat is a time of rest; no work may be done, and even cooking is forbidden. Meals must be prepared in advance or cooked with time-delay switches. Wine is drunk and challah, a special bread, is eaten. There are usually two loaves in memory of the double portion of manna that blessed the Israelites in the wilderness on the day before Shabbat. For Orthodox Jews, the term "rest" extends to not driving or taking public transportation. As they must walk to the synagogue on Shabbat, they live near their place of worship.

Far from being felt as a constraint, for many the Shabbat is welcomed as a relief from the weary pace of normal life, serving both to refresh and revitalize body and mind.

Rites of Passage

~ Birth: For Orthodox Jews, a baby is considered Jewish if born to a Jewish mother; the father's religion or ethnicity has no bearing. At eight days of age male babies are circumcised. This symbolizes their joining the covenant that God made with Abraham and his descendants. As soon as the child can speak, he is taught the words of the *shema*, the most important of all Jewish prayers.

~ Maturity: Bar Mitzvah, Bat Mitzvah. At the age of thirteen, a boy becomes a Bar Mitzvah, a son of the Covenant, and is now a responsible person who must follow Jewish Law, the *halakhot*, in its entirety. This is marked by the child reading from the Torah for the first time at the weekly synagogue service. This event is usually followed by a celebratory party. Reform Jews often perform the same rite, the Bat Mitzvah, for their daughters at the age of twelve.

~ Marriage: This is a holy covenant between the bride and the groom. Although usually performed by a rabbi with the synagogue cantor on hand to ensure that the spoken ceremony is conducted at an even pace, this duty may be performed by any layman in the presence of two witnesses. It usually takes place under an embroidered canopy, which represents the couple's future home.

At the end of the ceremony, the groom breaks a glass under his foot. This is to remind the couple that even times of great joy must be tempered by remembrance of the destruction of the Temple of Jerusalem.

~ Death: If death is near and the Jew is able, he or she speaks the words of the shema. If he is too ill, a friend or a relative will perform this last office for him. The funeral service is extremely simple. There are no prayers for the deceased, but *kaddish*, a prayer in praise of God, is said in their memory. Afterward there are seven days of private mourning for close relatives.

THE SYNAGOGUE

The Jewish home has always been the focus of prayer and ritual, and for some it still is. However, contemporary secular life intruding into the home, combined with the breakdown of the traditional family unit, has meant that the synagogue has become a more important center of Jewish life and worship.

The old-style synagogues at which many Orthodox Jews still worship have a central platform where the rabbi and cantor stand and the Torah is read. This

Above: Doorway of an old synagogue in Jerusalem

layout presumed the equality of all adult men, but not women. In Orthodox synagogues, women do not even sit with the men in the main body of the building but must worship from behind a partition or from a gallery. More liberal Jewish movements are inclusive to women and ordain female rabbis.

Newer-style synagogues have the platform at one end so that worshippers have become, as in Christian churches, more audience than participants.

WORSHIP

Jews face Jerusalem when praying, so synagogues have one wall facing in that direction. Set into it is an ark—a kind of cupboard—in which the Torah is kept. In Orthodox and sometimes Conservative synagogues, men wear a skull cap (*yarmelka* or *kippah*) or a hat, and married women wear a wig, hat, or scarf. This reminds them that they are always in the presence of God. Orthodox Jews may wear a head covering at all times.

Every day three basic prayers are said, in the morning, afternoon, and evening. These may be said in the synagogue or at home. Morning and evening synagogue services open with the shema prayer, which begins, "Hear O Israel, the Lord is our God, the Lord is One."

Morning services on the Shabbat, which include a sermon, psalms, and Bible readings, can last up to three hours, but normal services are generally less than an hour. The faithful speak the prayers out loud and are led by the cantor, who keeps a steady rhythm, although any capable layperson can replace him.

SEPHARDIC AND ASHKENAZI JEWS

The majority of the Jews in the world today are either Sephardim—from the Iberian Peninsula of Spain and Portugal—or Ashkenazim, from central Europe, in particular Germany and France, although in later times also from Poland and Russia. The principal difference between these two Jewish cultures was the religions of their host countries: Muslim for the former, Christian for the latter.

Sephardic Jews were subject to particular taxes and certain regulations that Muslims were spared, but they were not initially persecuted. There was no active theological hatred of their religious beliefs, and the Muslims hoped that in time they might come to see the error of their ways and accept Muhammad as their prophet. This enabled Sephardic Jews to participate in the culture of their host country, allowing them to develop a rich and unique intellectual tradition that synthesized Judaism with Greek philosophy and out of which sprang the Jewish mystical tradition of Kabbalah.

Their language is Ladino, a mixture of Spanish and Hebrew. The Sephardim were expelled from Spain by the Catholic Inquisition in 1492.

Ashkenazi Jews were much less fortunate. They were openly despised and always faced the danger of pogroms—bouts of organized violence—because the Christian church maintained that they must bear responsibility for the killing of Christ, and that they were allied to the devil. Unable to participate in surrounding cultural life, they lived in ghettos, and their intellectual studies were of necessity rabbinical. However, during the European Enlightenment, they emerged from the ghetto, and besides developing a rich culture of music and literature, were instrumental in the early formation of liberal and modern strands of Judaism. More recently, they have been the founders of Zionism and responsible for the establishment of the state of Israel. They speak Yiddish.

Left to right: *Some key figures in modern Jewish schools of thought: Solomon Schechter (1847–1915), Mordechai Kaplan (1881–1983), Zecharias Frankel (1801–75), and Abraham Geiger (1810–74)*

NONORTHODOX STRANDS OF MODERN JEWISH WORSHIP AND BELIEF

In the light of so much new secular knowledge in science, medicine, and technology; the changing role of women in society; and general cultural modernity, many Jews find that accepting the absolute authority of the Torah, as Orthodox Jews do, is no longer appropriate. They feel a need for radical reinterpretation.

Reform Jews

It was with Moses Mendelssohn (1729–86) and the Jewish Enlightenment that Judaism was first reinterpreted. For the first time, it was no longer the Torah that was the center of learning, but secular knowledge. Reform Jews do not define themselves through the suffering and persecution endured by the Jews in the past and are open to the contemporary cultural world.

They are inclusive of women, and accept children of Jewish fathers and Gentile mothers if they are brought up in the Jewish faith. Orthodox Jews do not see these children as Jewish, and refuse to accept the burgeoning numbers of Reform conversions, usually by Gentile marriage partners, as Jewish. This is causing a considerable rift in the fabric of the Jewish community and may not be healed for many years to come.

Conservative Jews

This movement aims to combine the best of Reform and Orthodoxy. Initiated in the late nineteenth and early twentieth centuries by Zecharias Frankel and Solomon Schechter, it preserves the traditional but accepts that Jewish Law may be

reinterpreted as modern circumstances and secular knowledge demand. Ritual is seen as less important than right, ethical behavior.

Reconstructionist Jews

Mordecai Kaplan and Ira Eisenstein, Americans in the 1920s, developed this branch of Judaism. Kaplan felt that the foremost problem in Jewish religion "is to take the Bible seriously, without taking it literally." Reconstructionist Judaism has reappraised the fundamentals, God, the Torah, and Israel, and is actively seeking to establish liberal Judaism in Israel. Inclusive, it involves women in synagogue services and, like Reform Judaism, accepts as Jewish children born of Jewish fathers and Gentile mothers.

Humanist Jews

Begun in the United States in the 1960s by Sherwin Wine, this form of Judaism is culturally, but not religiously, Jewish. It holds congregational meetings but believes problems may be solved without recourse to God. It welcomes anyone from any background who sincerely wants to share the Jewish experience.

CHRISTIANITY

Judaism, Islam, and Christianity are all scriptural religions, with a common ancestry in the Middle East. As such, they are monotheist religions, worshipping and insisting on the existence of one true God—both Judaism and Christianity look back to the revelation of Moses in the book of Exodus: "I am the God of thy father, the God of Abraham, the God of Isaac, and the God of Jacob." That same God, Christians avow, acted and spoke through the life and resurrection of Jesus Christ.

Starting out as a perceived renewal movement in Judaism, with Jesus identified as the long-awaited Messiah, or "anointed one," Christianity branched out from its parent religion, spread geographically, and diversified, so that it is today the most widespread of individual religions. There is a huge variety of forms, with different liturgies, rites, and practices, but all are bound by the common belief in Jesus as the son of God and as the way in which humankind can be reconciled to him.

CHRISTIAN SCRIPTURE

The Bible is the ultimate source of Christian doctrine, carried by the faithful, prominently located in churches, and studied by all devout believers. It is thought to be available in more than 400 languages around the world today.

The Christian Bible is made up of two elements: the Old Testament, which is the Hebrew Bible; and the New Testament, which covers the life, death, and resurrection of Jesus Christ and the subsequent activities of his followers.

The Hebrew Bible consists of four parts: The Law (known in Judaism as the Torah), the Historical books (Joshua to Esther), the Wisdom literature (Job to Song of Songs), and the books of the Prophets (Isaiah to Malachi). The Torah is also known as the Pentateuch: five books covering the history of the Hebrews from the creation of the world to the death of Moses. Central to the books is the act of Moses receiving the Tablets of the Law from God.

The New Testament contains four accounts of the life of Jesus Christ and are known as the Gospels, written by Matthew, Mark, Luke, and John, men traditionally called the evangelists. These texts were all written between the death of Jesus in 30 CE and the end of the first century: Mark's, the first, was written in 65 and John's was written last, in 95. The earliest Christian documents, however, predate these accounts in the form of the letters (Epistles) of Paul, who died in 65. His letters, and those of other apostles, are included in the New Testament together with the Acts of the Apostles (generally thought to have been written by Luke), which provide the history of the early Church in its first century and the missionary activities of the apostles.

The complete Bible has been translated into more than 400 languages; the New Testament has been translated into over 1,000 of the world's 6,500 languages.

The contents of the New Testament were not officially recognized until toward the end of the fourth century. The earliest listing of its twenty-seven books is in a letter by Athanasius, Bishop of Alexandria (*c.* 296–373), in 367. Meanwhile, oral accounts of the life of Jesus circulated well after the writing of the New Testament, and in the first two centuries of the Christian era there were many translations from the Greek into Latin, as well as Armenian, Coptic, and Syriac. To attempt a reconciliation of the various translations and traditions, in 382 Pope Damasus held a council to decide the canon of books in the Old and New Testaments; and in 404 Jerome (*c.* 342–420) completed his translation of the Bible into Latin. This, known as the Vulgate, became the church's standard edition of the Bible. Its status was confirmed by the Roman Catholic Church at the Council of Trent in 1546.

It was not until the sixteenth century and the Reformation that translations were made into commonly spoken languages, as new Protestant churches sprang up in the nations of northern Europe. There have subsequently been many versions of the Bible, some aimed at specific readerships, such as children, others written in everyday language to overcome the "antique" style of the authorized version.

In the Bible, there is no sense that the text is the actual word of God (as with the Qur'an, for example) and all translations and versions may be regarded rather as interpretations, each translator making specific decisions about meanings. Certain passages have become corrupted by the renewal process of ecclesiastical transcribing over the centuries. However, it has always been seen as the message of God, and ever since the Reformation, the Bible has played a central role in Protestantism—for personal salvation and moral teaching, God's guidance can be sought within the Bible in almost any situation.

As the Middle Ages gave way to the modern age, many of the accepted truths of the Bible were challenged in the light of archaeology and scientific research. Although most Christians saw the contents of the Bible as the sole source of divine truth until recent centuries, the development of science—such as Galileo's confirmation that the earth orbits the sun, as well as new discoveries about astronomy, the age of the earth, and evolution—began to erode its perceived literal truth. The challenge of the scientists led to many controversies and confrontations. While the majority of people today accept the scientific view of such matters as evolution, there exists a powerful lobby based on "biblicism," which proclaims the infallibility of the book as the word of God and demands that creationism be included in school curricula as well. Thus is true especially in America, where the Bible has played a major role in the development of Christian churches.

THE ESSENCE OF CHRISTIANITY

Christianity is monotheistic: it asserts that there is one God, creator of the universe and all living things. He is transcendent and immanent—not of the material universe yet at the same time pervading and sustaining it. Christians regard him as a paternal figure, often calling him "Father," in the way Jesus did.

Sin

Christians believe that God created humankind in his own image, promising them immortality and participation in the divine nature. But what separates humanity from God is sin. According to the book of Genesis in the Old Testament, God placed the first humans, Adam and Eve, in the paradise of the Garden of Eden, but forbade them to eat the fruit of the tree of knowledge of good and evil. Their disobedience was the source of *peccatum originis*, original sin. As punishment they became mortal, and the sin was a burden to be carried by all humankind (with the exception of Jesus and his mother, Mary), from generation to generation. Humans are thus born into a state of original sin.

This concept of original sin was powerful. It was formalized in the Western Church by Augustine, but from the eighteenth century onward it has generally been replaced by the idea that human beings are inherently incapable of living a sin-free life on their own; they need God's help, and it is only by means of the death and resurrection of Jesus that humankind can be saved. At its core, Christianity is thus a religion of redemption.

Jesus Christ

Christians believe that some two thousand years ago God sent his only son, Jesus, to earth in human form. As prophesied in the Old Testament, he lived, taught God's message of love and forgiveness, was crucified, died, and rose from the dead. By this he atoned for the sins of humanity, attaining victory over evil and death—death's triumph at the crucifixion was reversed as Christ rose victorious in resurrection.

Anselm (c. 1033–1109) rationalized this process, and his explanation has been accepted by both Catholics and Protestants.

As he explains, if God's justice is to uphold the moral order of the universe, human sin cannot be ignored. However, in his mercy, God sought to restore humankind to the way he originally intended. So God became Man in Christ, and the death of Christ satisfied God's justice, which can be applied to all humanity.

Thus Jesus brought about the forgiveness of sins and reconciliation with God for all who believe. Eventually, he will return to save believers at the end of the world, and will be God's agent at the Last Judgment.

THE HOLY TRINITY

God is also seen as the Trinity, "one God in three persons." It consists of:

~ **The Father, the Creator**

~ **Jesus Christ, Son of God,** who thus has both a divine and a human nature

~ **The Holy Spirit, or Holy Ghost,** the power of God that infuses all Christians, supporting and sustaining them. Augustine saw the Holy Spirit as the bond of unity within the Trinity. In the Acts of the Apostles it descended upon the disciples (at the Feast of Pentecost), giving them the power to teach the word of the Lord in many languages.

These three are equal and of one substance. The Trinity is perhaps the least understood aspect of Christianity, and the element that causes Muslims to assert that Christianity is not a monotheistic religion.

The Nature of Jesus

In the early centuries of Christianity, there was considerable speculation as to the exact nature of Jesus and his relationship to God. While he could be seen as the manifestation of God in human form, did he have a fully divine dimension? Christians today generally agree that Jesus was fully God and fully human, yet Jesus addressed God as "Father." So was he in some way separate from him? Was he created by God? Much speculation led to controversies and beliefs that were declared heretical, some of which persist to the present day. The Council of Chalcedon in 451 concluded that Jesus has two natures, one divine, one human, so that he is both one in God and one in humankind and thus able to mediate between them.

Ethics and Behavior

Christianity did not deviate from the Ten Commandments of the Old Testament, which set out the rules by which to live a righteous life, but in the New Testament Jesus was asked by the Pharisees which was the greatest commandment in the Law. He answered that the first was to love God; the second was to love one another: "Thou shalt love thy neighbor as thyself" (Mark 12:31). Love is the central essence of Christianity, the love of God and the love of one's fellow human being. In this spirit, Christians believe that unbelievers and sinners can yet be saved, which is why evangelism has always been a strong element of Christianity.

CHRISTIAN WORSHIP

There are two fundamental rites common to all denominations of the Christian faith: baptism and the practice known variously as Mass, Holy Communion, or the Eucharist.

Baptism

This is initiation into the Christian faith, carried out when a person converts to Christianity; often in the West it is an infant's formal induction into the Church. The practice began at least as early as the second century.

Its origins lie in the Jewish practice for converts to Judaism but especially in the baptism of Jesus in the river Jordan by John the Baptist. At baptism, the individual repents, is "washed clean" of sin, and receives the Holy Spirit. (According to Paul it also symbolizes union with the risen Jesus and incorporation into the "body of Christ.") Today baptism is still sometimes by total immersion, but in denominations where in-font baptism is performed, the baby is baptized with the ritual pouring of water on its forehead from a special basin, or font, in the church. In addition, there may be adult sponsors, known as godparents, who promise to guide and support the newly baptized in the Christian faith.

The Eucharist

This is the reenactment of events at the Last Supper, Jesus' last meal with his disciples before his arrest and execution. Jesus blessed bread and wine and offered it to his disciples, telling them to eat and drink, and that "this is my body" and "this is my blood." This is reenacted in churches: bread (usually replaced by a wafer) and wine are blessed, and each member of the congregation partakes, the officiating priest saying, as appropriate, "the body or Christ" and "the blood of Christ."

For Roman Catholics, who call the sacrament Mass, consecration turns the substance, or inner reality, of the bread and wine into the actual body and blood of Jesus, while their outer, physical character remains unchanged. This is known as transubstantiation, defined at the 1215 Lateran Council and reaffirmed at the Council of Trent in 1551. In the Eastern Orthodox and Anglican churches (the latter calling the rite Holy Communion), transubstantiation is not considered; Lutheran churches believe in consubstantiation, the coexistence of the body and blood with the complete physical elements. For Protestants, Jesus is present in spirit and power, so the service is symbolic and a communal expression of the communion of worshippers; indeed, some Protestant churches consider it to be simply a faith-enhancing memorial, while the Quakers do not practice it at all.

Prayer

Prayer may be observed for a wide variety of reasons, including intercession or petition, penitence, thanksgiving, and adoration. According to the New Testament, Jesus instituted various practices, including baptism, the Lord's Supper (Eucharist), the casting out of demons, and so on. These led to the formal liturgical customs of Christian prayer, Divine Office, and the concept of sacrament—in addition to private prayer or devotion.

The Sacraments

The classic definition of a sacrament is "an outward and visible sign conveying an inward and spiritual grace." The actual Church practices remained fluid into the second millennium of the Christian era, until Peter Lombard (c. 1100–60) set forth the structure of the sacraments in about 1155. These were codified by Thomas Aquinas (c. 1225–74) and confirmed at the Council of Trent in 1545–63.

For the Church of England, services are set out in the Book of Common Prayer, first imposed by the Act of Uniformity in 1549 and revised in 1552. (At that time, absence from church was punishable, as was attending other forms of religious service.) The 1662 Act, after a period of religious upheaval and the coutnry's civil wars, required all ministers to assent to the Book of Common Prayer—about 2,000 Presbyterian ministers who refused were ejected from their livings. The book specifies daily offices, including morning prayers, Evensong (evening prayers), and other sacraments.

Above: St. Patrick's Cathedral is the seat of the Roman Catholic diocese of New York. Here Archbishop Edwin F. O'Brien conducts Mass.

THE SEVEN SACRAMENTS

~ **Baptism**

~ **Penance:** Reconciliation or confession. The Fourth Lateran Council of 1215 required every Christian to confess his or her sins at least once a year. This developed from a rigorous system into today's "private penance," whereby spoken penance is normal, an adherent making anonymous private confession in a special cubicle to a priest, who awards appropriate penance, usually today in the form of recitation.

~ **Eucharist:** The greatest sacrament.

~ **Confirmation:** Appropriate only for the baptized, confirmation makes a person a "perfect Christian," whereby the grace of God is more fully conveyed and baptismal promises are renewed. Among most Christian churches, Holy Communion can only be administered to the confirmed, and there is normally a course of instruction preceding the sacrament.

~ **Matrimony:** The priest does not actually confer matrimony but witnesses the couple's vows, which are made before God.

~ **Ordination:** Induction into holy orders.

~ **Extreme Unction:** Anointing the dying, with the expression of penance and preparation for death.

Right: *Paris's great cathedral, Notre Dame, built between 1163 and 1182. The west front was added in 1200–20.*

CHRISTIAN FESTIVALS

The feasts of the Christian world are centered on events in the life of Jesus but are sometimes connected with the seasons. Immovable feasts include commemorations of martyrs' and saints' days, and by the fourth century there were several major fixed feasts, including Christmas. Note that the use of the Julian calendar in the Eastern Orthodox Church results in dates that vary from those in the West, where the Gregorian calendar of 1582 is used. (Protestant countries were slow to adopt the new calendar, England only changing in 1752.) As in many other religions, other principal feast days are determined by phases of the moon.

THE CHRISTIAN CALENDAR

~ **Sunday** is the Christian sabbath, commemorating the resurrection of Christ, which took place on the first day of the week, and it is still the principal day of the week for Christian worship around the world. It is mentioned as having been celebrated by St. Paul and officially became a day of rest in the fourth century. In 321, Emperor Constantine forbade work on this day, and until the thirteenth century attending Mass on Sundays was strictly enforced. Since then there has been gradual relaxation, although sabbatarian movements have fought against this.

~ **Advent** (coming) begins the Liturgical Year, and is a season of preparation for Christmas (and for the Second Coming). It starts on November 30 or the Sunday nearest to St. Andrew's Day.

~ **Christmas**, December 25, commemorates the nativity of Christ. The actual date of his birth is not known (nor, indeed, is the exact year), but the date was probably chosen to oppose the pagan festival of Natalis Solis Invicti in the Roman Empire. Observance spread from Rome—in the Eastern church, Epiphany is seen as more important. It is celebrated by three Masses: at midnight, dawn, and during the day. From the nineteenth century onward the Christmas season has become longer and increasingly secularized, seen especially as a time of family reunion and gift-giving. It is now the major retail season of the year in many countries around the world.

~ **Epiphany** (manifestation) was introduced in the West during the fourth century. It falls on January 6 and commemorates the presentation of the infant Jesus in the Temple. More popularly, it is connected with the first Gentiles to believe in the Christ: the Magi (wise men), whose story in the New Testament involves the search for the infant by following a star and their presentation to him of gifts of gold, frankincense, and myrrh.

~ **Lent** (spring) is a season of forty days preceding Easter and is a time of penitence and fasting; a Mass is celebrated each day. In the West it became a period of abstinence and alms-giving. It begins with Ash Wednesday. In Eastern Orthodox churches, icons are traditionally covered or taken down during this period.

~ **Palm Sunday** begins **Holy** or **Passion Week**, which remembers the last days of Jesus' life. This day commemorates his triumphal entry to Jerusalem, when according to the New Testament crowds threw down palm leaves before him.

~ **Maundy** or **Holy Thursday** is the Thursday before Easter and celebrates the Last Supper. It is marked by alms-giving and a ceremonial form of feet-washing (*pedilavium*) in memory of Jesus' washing of the disciples' feet (symbolic of humbleness and equality) before the Last Supper.

~ **Good Friday** is the Friday before Easter and the anniversary of the Crucifixion; it is a day of penance, abstinence, and fasting. The tradition of a procession on the Via Dolorosa (Way of Grief) between the Stations of the Cross, traditionally Christ's route to his crucifixion, began in Jerusalem. In the fourteenth century, the Franciscans began tracing this route, and this led to the tradition of reenacting the holy procession, which is copied in other places, most notably in Rome.

~ **Easter** is the greatest festival of the Christian year, a day of joy recalling the resurrection of Jesus Christ. Its date was fixed at the Council of Nicaea in 325 as the first Sunday following the full moon after the vernal equinox, and this may vary between March 22 and April 25 (the method of fixing the date has often been disputed). In the Eastern Orthodox churches a "new fire" is brought into the church, symbolizing Jesus, as the light of the world, banishing the darkness of death. The giving of eggs at Easter is a pre-Christian practice.

~ **Ascension** is the fortieth day after Easter (the Resurrection) and celebrates Jesus' withdrawal to heaven as witnessed by the apostles.

~ **Pentecost** is the fiftieth day after Easter and is popularly called Whitsunday. It marks the day when the Holy Spirit descended upon the apostles, enabling them to preach in tongues so that all nations might understand. It is, after Easter, the most important of the Christian church festivals.

~ **Annunciation** is on March 25, commemorating the revelation to the Virgin Mary that she would bear the Son of God.

Saints' Days. Saints are people revered because of their lives and ability to perform miracles. Saints are not worshipped but asked for intercession because they are close to God, owing to their holiness, and may intercede for the living. Patron saints are those believed to protect and aid specific causes, occupations, or countries. Each saint has a day in the calendar, and in Roman Catholic countries these days are celebrated as public holidays, and there may be processions and street celebrations.

THE ROMAN CATHOLIC CHURCH

The largest of the Christian churches by far, the Roman Catholic Church has about a billion adherents (nearly half of whom live in South America) and more than 400,000 priests worldwide. Highly organized, it is led by a hierarchy of bishops and priests, with the pope at their head. He is seen as the successor to the apostle St. Peter, who was martyred in Rome around 64 CE, and is elected to office for a life term by the College of Cardinals. The pope is also the political head of the Vatican, a tiny secular state within the city of Rome, whose independence was recognized by the Italian government in the 1929 Lateran Treaty. This is in fact the remnant of a larger territory, the Papal States, which until the Italian Risorgimento (unification) in the mid-nineteenth century stretched across the Italian peninsula.

The Roman Catholic Church stresses its centrality and continuity of belief, liturgy, and structure from the early Church—*catholic* means "universal"—despite two great splits in Christian ecclesiastical history, in 1054 (see pages 48–49) and in the sixteenth century (see pages 60–62).

In modern times some aspects of Catholic doctrine have caused tensions, especially in the light of modernizing movements in other churches. However, there is an increasingly ecumenical side to Catholicism today, and efforts are being made to improve relationships with other churches. The Catholic Church has made a firm commitment to education worldwide, and has always been strongly evangelical (especially in the case of Spain from the sixteenth to eighteenth centuries). With its deep historic roots and powerful organizational structure, Catholicism offers a stable, authoritative belief system and community that has lost none of its attraction in a changing and often uncertain world.

THE CHURCH OF ROME

~ Catholics believe that **tradition** is a major source of faith in addition to scripture, which Protestants maintain is the sole source.

~ Catholics adhere to the **Seven Sacraments**, while Protestants recognize just two essential sacraments: baptism and the Eucharist. For Catholics, attendance at **Mass** on Sundays and certain feast days is mandatory.

~ The **visible aspect** of Catholicism is strikingly different from that of its Protestant counterparts. It is strongly sacramental, with much splendor and pomp. Catholic churches and cathedrals are richly decorated and gilded.

~ Catholics believe in **transubstantiation** at the Eucharist (see page 104).

~ Until modern times, the liturgy and Bible for Catholics were in **Latin**, and it was eventually conceded that this placed a barrier between the faithful (especially in a literate age) and the doctrines of the Church. Since Vatican II, the liturgy is in the vernacular and the Bible is accepted in many languages.

~ **Celibacy** is required for priests.

~ **Women** cannot be ordained.

~ The use of artificial **contraceptives** is forbidden.

~ **Abortion** is not allowed.

~ **Divorce** is not recognized.

~ **Saints** are venerated, and the cult of the **Blessed Virgin Mary** figures large in Catholic worship; these aspects are rejected by Protestants.

~ Vatican I (see page 71) asserted the primacy and infallibility of the **pope** concerning matters of faith and morality.

THE EASTERN ORTHODOX CHURCH

Known variously as the Eastern, Greek, or Greco-Roman Church, this is a family of churches sharing a common background, history, and doctrine. It consists of the ancient Patriarchates of Constantinople, Alexandria, Antioch, and Jerusalem together with the churches of Eastern Europe. It has also spread widely to Finland, Japan, China, Korea, and Africa. Each church is independent, but together they form a community of churches, acknowledging the primacy of the Patriarch of Constantinople (also known as the Ecumenical Patriarch, a style dating from the sixth century). There is, however, no overarching jurisdiction as with Rome; Russia, the largest of these churches, is the most influential.

The Orthodox Church sees itself as the direct heir to the church of the Byzantine Empire. In the first millennium of Christianity there was just one Christian church, but tensions between the eastern patriarchates and the See of Rome grew with the centuries. The tensions culminated in a break between the two churches, the Great Schism, traditionally dated to 1054, when both sides engaged in retaliatory excommunications; after centuries of negotiation, it was formalized in 1484.

Inherently conservative, the doctrine of the Orthodox church is based upon the decisions of the first seven Ecumenical Councils and the writings of the early church fathers. Monasteries are important in the Orthodox Church, providing spiritual and intellectual leadership. Mount Athos, a theocratic republic in northeastern Greece, is the principal monastic community, founded in 962 by St. Athanasius the Athonite (c. 920–1003). There are now some thirty monasteries in the complex at the "Holy Mountain."

THE EASTERN ORTHODOX CHURCH

~ The Seven Sacraments are recognized but called **Mysteries**.
~ Services are not in Latin or Greek but in the **language** of the population, albeit often in an archaic form.
~ **Baptism** is by immersion, and children take communion from an early age.
~ Worship is often **candlelit**, and the worshippers do not sit in pews.
~ In the Orthodox Church, the sanctuary and altar are normally separated from the main body of the church by a screen, the **iconostasis**, beyond which only the priests can pass.
~ **Icons** provide the most immediately distinctive element in Orthodox churches. These are images of Jesus, the Virgin Mary, or saints painted on wood, or perhaps as mosaics or carved in ivory. They are held to be sacred and are venerated; the image invokes the presence of the subject to which the worshipper can pray. Such images, which are often displayed in homes, are seen as powerful channels of divine grace and are much loved. (See pages 44 and 46 for discussion of the iconoclasm controversy of the eighth and ninth centuries.)

Left: St. Peter's Cathedral in the Vatican was built between 1506 and 1626 and is located on the supposed site of St. Peter's crucifixion.

Right: The Savior on the Blood Cathedral, St. Petersburg, was built on the site of the assassination of Tsar Alexander II in 1881.

THE ANGLICAN COMMUNION

The Anglican Communion is a group of churches, each autonomous but deriving from the Church of England. Collegiate in structure, the thirty-seven Anglican churches share a common liturgy and a number recognize the leadership of the archbishop of Canterbury. They meet every ten years at Lambeth, in London, but decisions made at these conferences are not binding on individual churches.

The Christian church in England was established in 597 by St. Augustine, who founded the See of Canterbury, absorbing the ancient Celtic church over the next century. The church lay outside papal jurisdiction until the Norman conquest of England in 1066, when it became part of the Roman Catholic Church. The Church of England emerged in the early sixteenth century when King Henry VIII broke with the papacy in order to divorce his first wife, Catherine of Aragon. Henry was not in favor of the doctrinal and sacramental changes implicit in the Reformation; his resistance to that movement had earned him the title of "Defender of the Faith" from the pope, following his *Assertio Septem Sacramentorum* of 1521, which defended the Seven Sacraments. During the 1530s, Henry made himself head of the Church of England and also dissolved the monasteries in England with the 1534 Act of Supremacy, but it was not until the reign of his son, Edward VI, that the actual Protestant Reformation in England began.

His successor, Mary, reversed the reforms, and one of its chief architects, Archbishop Thomas Cranmer (1489–1556), was one of many burned at the stake for heresy. Mary's death curtailed re-Romanization, and during the reign of Elizabeth I (1558–1603) the Church of England emerged as Protestant, rejecting transubstantiation, clerical celibacy, and all but two of the Seven Sacraments, while resting doctrine on the scriptures, ecclesiastical authority, and reason. Traditional liturgy was enshrined in the Book of Common Prayer (1549, revised in 1552), while an English edition of the Bible was already in place in the form of Miles Coverdale's *Great Bible*. It was followed in 1611 by the Authorized, King James Version.

The Anglican Communion remains broad, encompassing a parochial freedom that allows for practices and attitudes (particularly in the "High Church" epitomized by the Oxford Movement in the early nineteenth century) that approach Catholicism. Since 2002, for example, divorcees are allowed to remarry in church. This toleration, however, has tested the church during recent years, particularly over the questions of the ordination of women and homosexuality. In 1992 the General Synod accepted the ordination of women priests; there were many in the church who couldn't reconcile to this, and during the 1990s there were defections to Catholicism. This rift was exacerbated by the election in 2006 of a woman bishop in the Episcopal Church of America. Additionally, the question of homosexuality reached crisis point in 2003 when the Episcopal Church of America elected an openly gay bishop (see page 80).

THE MEMBER CHURCHES OF THE ANGLICAN COMMUNION

In the British Isles:
~ The Church of England, which is the established church of the realm. The British monarch is the Supreme Governor, and the bishops sit in the upper chamber of Parliament.
~ The Church of Ireland
~ The Church in Wales
~ The Episcopal Church in Scotland
Most countries of the Commonwealth, formerly the British Empire, and the Protestant Episcopal Church of the United States of America, are also members. Churches have also been founded in China, Japan, and other countries.

LUTHERANISM

By the end of the sixteenth century, two-thirds of the German population had accepted Lutheranism, and it became the state religion in the Scandinavian countries and Prussia. Following Luther's precepts as set out in the 1580 *Book of Concord*, the doctrine stresses justification by faith and scripture as the sole basis of belief, with the sermon central to services, and the liturgy in vernacular language.

Lutherans were part of the colonial movement to the New World in the sixteenth and seventeenth centuries, where they founded new churches. Migrants to America during the nineteenth century and early twentieth century swelled their numbers greatly and included people from a wide variety of European nations, so while Lutheran churches in the United States grew in number, they tended for first-language reasons to become grouped by national origin.

The churches retain their independence but have organized councils to cooperate on particular issues. In 1967, the Lutheran Council in the United States of America was founded, encompassing four major churches that comprised 95 percent of the nation's Lutherans. The Lutheran World Federation was established in Switzerland in 1947 and now has its headquarters at Geneva, representing over 50 million Lutherans. It is principally involved in social welfare, missionary, and educational projects and exercises no jurisdiction over the individual churches and their congregations. In the modern atmosphere of ecumenicalism, in 1999 the Lutheran World Federation and the Vatican agreed on a common statement concerning justification by faith.

CONGREGATIONALISM

Congregational churches insist upon the autonomy of local churches or congregations and constitute the oldest sect of nonconformists. They began in England as independent groups meeting in the mid-sixteenth century to preach and worship in separation from the newly established Church of England, their ministers elected within congregations. Driven underground by persecution, they reemerged in the mid-seventeenth century, where, as Independents, they formed the backbone of Cromwell's Army during the Civil Wars. Like the Presbyterians, they have always been anticentralist, but nevertheless found it useful to form local associations for mutual support and aid. They preached that:

~ Each congregation should be independent, electing its own ministers.

~ Jesus Christ is the sole head of the church.

~ The church has no relationship with the state.

~ The Bible is the only source of authority.

Persecution forced them to flee, and a number sailed on the *Mayflower* to New England, where they flourished. Instead of the Anglican church, Congregationalism became the established church in Massachussetts and Connecticut.

Right: *John Knox (c. 1513–73) was instrumental in establishing the Reformed Church of Scotland on essentially Calvinist lines in 1559. Presbyterianism was established as the state church during the civil wars.*

PRESBYTERIAN CHURCHES

The Presbyterian churches constitute English-speaking versions of the Calvinist-inspired Reformed churches and see themselves as in direct continuity from apostolic times, and their churches are based on the apostolic model in the New Testament. For Presbyterians, the word of God, as expounded in the Bible, is the supreme standard of faith. The church is a community of equals with Jesus Christ as its head. Following Calvinism, it rejects the hierarchy of bishops and instead officers of the church are elected representatives of the people; church government is undertaken by assemblies. The central priestly role is taken by a presbyter (a title of a Christian minister, lower in rank than a bishop but superior to a deacon, dating from the second century) now more commonly known as an elder.

Independently minded, Presbyterians have often disagreed, and the church has been prone to division on such questions as the relationship between church and state, and such doctrinal issues as predestination.

Presbyterians in England trace their origins to the Puritans of the mid-sixteenth century, communities pressing for the abolition of the episcopacy in the newly established Church of England. In America,

Above: *The wood-built Methodist church at Cades Cove in the Smoky Mountains of Tennessee. Such churches reflect the unostentatious, simple style typical of many Protestant denominations.*

Presbyterianism is associated with the Pilgrim fathers and Puritans escaping from religious oppression in Britain. In 1706 settler churches began to form loosely organized presbyteries, which ten years later expanded into a synod. Scottish and Irish immigrants swelled their numbers, and in 1789 the first general assembly took place in Philadelphia.

BAPTIST CHURCHES

One of the largest of Protestant churches in the world today, Baptists feel that only believers—not infants—can be baptized, and are baptized by immersion. It is a doctrine that can be traced back to the Anabaptists, sixteenth-century groups in Switzerland, Moravia, Germany, and the Low Countries.

It was in the United States that the Baptist movement made its greatest mark, growing to be one of the great Christian churches there today. The Great Awakening provided a massive impetus to the growth of Baptist communities, especially in the South, but in the nineteenth century slavery split the churches. Meanwhile the black communities of America took to the movement. After the Civil War, freed slaves made Baptist churches the centers of their communities' spiritual and social lives, and by the latter part of the twentieth century, Baptists in the United States accounted for two-thirds of the black Christian community.

Baptists follow a congregational form of administration, essentially democratic and fiercely independent. During the twentieth century there was fragmentation into hundreds of independent churches, but these remain voluntarily linked for various cooperative ventures. In the nineteenth century, the strict Calvinism was modified and communion is now practiced in most Baptist churches. For some churches, the Bible is literally the word of God, while for others it is subject to interpretation in a modern context. Sermons about scriptural passages are the most important elements of services, accompanied by spontaneous prayer and singing of hymns.

QUAKERS

The Religious Society of Friends was founded in the mid-seventeenth century by George Fox (1624–91), who had become disenchanted at the hypocrisy he saw in the established church. He began preaching in England in 1647 and rapidly found a following. His main tenet was that churches, chapels, and cathedrals were unnecessary, as were ordained priests and the sacraments. Christ's teaching was immediate and should be applied to the whole of one's life—all one needed to do

was wait silently for the "inner light," the inward knowledge of salvation, the internal apprehension of God. Practically alone of all Christian denominations, Quakers did not practice the sacraments and believed in spiritual baptism and spiritual communion. The movement spread by the 1650s to much of Britain and Ireland, parts of Europe, and then to the New World.

Quakers have been great reformers and campaigners on many important issues, in addition to their missionary work— including temperance, women's rights, the abolition of slavery, prison reform, the abolition of the death penalty, and the care of the mentally ill—and have been in the forefront of educational and relief work. In 1947 the American and English Family Service Councils jointly received the Nobel Peace Prize for their efforts during World War II and after.

METHODISM

In 1738 John Wesley (1703–91), an ordained minister of the Church of England, became a fervent evangelist, determined to save souls and bring the message of Christianity to those parts of society that seemed to have been neglected by the state church. He began to conduct evangelist outdoor meetings, and he visited the big cities, where the Industrial Revolution was creating vast slums.

Lay recruits joined him, and the movement grew, based first on itinerant lay speakers, then on local chapels. Methodism introduced a practical, no-nonsense means of bringing salvation through Jesus Christ, instilling hope and a sense of worth in the masses. It shares many of the values of Presbyterianism and lays emphasis on the power of the Holy Spirit; the heart of Christianity is one's personal relationship with God. Without insistence on doctrinal conformity or interest in theological speculation, there are wide variations in beliefs and practices.

Wesley was also a great educator, seeking to bring learning to those for whom books and education were not otherwise available; he introduced church magazines, cheap books, and reading rooms and set up Sunday schools. Missionary work has always been a central aspect of Methodism, and the church participated in the founding of the London Missionary Society in 1795, along with the Congregational, Anglican, and Presbyterian churches.

In 1784 Wesley consecrated Dr. Thomas Coke as a missionary to America, and Coke founded the independent Methodist Episcopal Church. It grew rapidly as an episcopal church and by the mid-nineteenth century Methodism had more members than any other denomination.

Above: As John Wesley's preaching powers grew, his sermons had great emotional effect on the listeners. He had no intention of challenging or entering conflict with the Church of England; rather, he saw Methodism as supplementary, reaching parts of the community the established church seemed to have passed by.

PENTECOSTALISM

The core of Pentecostalism lies in "believer baptism," a mystical experience identified with the events of the first Pentecost when the Holy Spirit descended on Jesus' disciples, bringing them the gift of speaking in tongues so that they could preach to foreigners in their own languages. The Pentecostal movement teaches that all Christians should seek this experience, when they might also receive the gift of prophecy, or the ability to heal the sick or to exorcise evil spirits. (Illness is seen as caused by sin, which can be cured by releasing the soul of the victim from the clutches of the devil, as Jesus is recorded in the Gospels to have done many times.)

The movement began in 1901 at Topeka, Kansas, when the first case of speaking in tongues was seen, and an evangelical movement grew from this incident. The movement was phenomenally successful and many churches were established in the United States, Europe, and Africa.

Pentecostalism is transdenominational, with thousands of churches worldwide, and it is still growing—it is believed to be the world's fastest-growing Christian movement today, with wide appeal, particularly to the underprivileged. The emotional charisma of the minister is vital. There is no prescribed form of worship, and this lack of structure is welcoming, releasing believers from their everyday lives to experience with others what they see to be the true knowledge of Jesus in a warm atmosphere of fellowship.

A similar movement within the Roman Catholic Church, known as Charismatic Renewal, began in 1967 in Pittsburgh, Pennsylvania; it was accorded legitimacy at Vatican II and has received continued papal support.

ISLAM

Now in its fourteenth century, the religion of Islam seems to be surrounded by controversy and conflict, and the troubles affecting Islam are constantly in the news. It has not always been so. The belief system taught by Muhammad ibn Abd Allah during the early years of the seventh century was spread with incredible speed in the wake of dramatic military conquests. Within a hundred years, Islam was the religion of a huge empire stretching from the Atlantic to the gates of India, and in the centuries following there blossomed a culture that added immeasurably to the civilization of the world.

ISLAMIC SCRIPTURE

The Qur'an

Muslims see the Qur'an (which means "the recitation") as God's final guidance for humanity, setting forth the unaltered words of God as revealed to Muhammad at Mecca and Medina. It is unique, universal, and eternal, covering all aspects of life with no separation between the sacred and the secular.

The message of God covers a wide range of content and is expressed by means of parables, allegories, texts covering the law, as well as ecstatic passages. Included are the beliefs and creed of Islam; God's guidance to humankind on all moral and social aspects of life; the law; and the history of previous nations and prophets.

There is no chronological order to the Qur'an; some translations out of Arabic have attempted to remedy this, but none is thought satisfactory. Indeed, it is still a matter of opinion whether the book can be faithfully translated at all. Converts to Islam within the Muslim empire learned to read it in Arabic, which helped to spread that language and made "Arabs" out of a multiplicity of ethnicities.

It is divided into 114 *suras*, each comprised of more than 6,000 verses, each sura beginning with the phrase "In the Name of Allah, the Beneficent, the Merciful." The suras dating from Muhammad's time in Mecca include the fundamental messages: the unity of God, the obedience due to him from humankind, and God's works from creation (*khalq*) to the Last Day of Judgment. The revelations at Medina tend to concern themselves with more social and legal issues.

The revelations came to Muhammad over an extended period, perhaps a score of years, and they came in no specific order. They were memorized and written down on materials that were on hand at the time, including stones, cloth, and palm leaves. But after his death, variations became apparent, so the first of Muhammad's successors, or caliphs, Abu Bakr, put together an official compilation and sent official copies to all important Muslim regions of the time. This was not easy, as the Arabic script was evolving. More refinements were introduced to facilitate the reading of the Qur'an without touchng the text during the seventh and eighth centuries. Seven ways to recite the Qur'an are accepted as canonical by Muslim scholars.

Muhammad was not, of course, the author of the Qur'an; instead the book is deemed "uncreated," having preexisted the world. The words are those of God. Muhammad was God's Prophet, the last in a series of messengers sent by God to deliver his message to humankind. *Nabi* (Prophet) is the term used by Muslims to identify those sent by God to communicate with humanity; of these, *rasuls* (messengers) were sent with

new sets of divine laws and revelations. The Qur'an mentions 313 such messengers, many of whom appear in the Bible. More than ten works of revelation were made, including those to Adam, Seth, Enoch, and Abraham, but those have been lost. The works of Moses and Jesus survive—though, according to Muslim belief, in a corrupted form. The Qur'an recognizes three other revealed scriptures that survive, each God's blueprint for living according to his law: *Tawrat*, the Torah, given to Moses; *Zabur*, the Psalms, revealed to David; and *Injil*, the Gospel, revealed to Jesus.

Jews and Christians were accused of corrupting the earlier revelations, changing the text, or deliberately misinterpreting it; so the Qur'an, in contrast, is final and perfect, and supplants all earlier revelations. It is the last and definitive version, the repository of perfect truth (and, at Jesus' Second Coming, he will judge people by the law of the Qur'an rather than by the Gospels). For this reason, Muhammad is said to be the Seal of Prophets; he is the last, and the message he brought will never be replaced. There will be no further revelations.

Above: *Before reading the Qur'an, Muslims are supposed to perform* ghusl, *major ablution, cleansing the body in pure water.*

Hadith

Additional to the Qur'an are the Hadith, the sayings and deeds of Muhammad, who is regarded as *Insan al-Kamil*, "the perfect man," and thus an exemplar for all Islam. *Hadith qudsi* include the words of God, directly spoken, but mediated by Muhammad, while Hadiths are the words of the Prophet.

After the death of Muhammad, Muslims would often face decisions by asking, "What would the Prophet do?" The Hadith are seen as texts that explain the Qur'an and offer practical examples from which Muslims can take guidance. As such they became *sunna* (literally, "the path"), guides to conduct that are seen as the proper behavior for a Muslim. The sunna were codified into Hadith collections during the eighth and ninth centuries.

The problem that arose with the Hadith involved reliability, which the Prophet himself was at pains to point out. While the words of the Qur'an are the immaculate, unaltered words of God, the Hadith relies upon reported speech and actions. By the ninth century, a vast amount of material existed purporting to be hadiths, some of which were invented. Particularly in the realm of *shari'ah* (the law), it was found necessary to verify the authenticity of sayings or actions in the Hadith, and there evolved a new branch of Islamic scholarship, *Ilm al-Rijal* or *Al-Jarh wal taa'dil* (the biographies of men) by which the provenance of a saying could be traced, usually by the careful checking of the "chain" of transmitters, in order to solve disagreements about interpretation and application. A hadith must also, of course, be in keeping with the words of the Qur'an. Most popular are the Six Books of Hadiths. The two *Sahihs* (sound collections) of Imam Muhammad b. Isma'il al-Bukhari (810–70) and Muslim b. al-Hajjaj (d. 875) are held to be the most authoritative; each contains some 7,500 hadiths. The other collections accepted as genuine by almost all Muslims are those of Abu Dawud (d. 888), al-Nasa'i (d. 915), al-Tirmidhi (d. 892) and Ibn Majah (d. 886).

Together the Qur'an and sunna comprise the two basic sources for Islam and provide the rules whereby humans relate with God and the means by which they are to carry out his *Shari'ah* (wishes). All else is commentary.

THE ESSENCE OF ISLAM

Islam means peace, a peace attained by surrender and allegiance to God. It is the final revelation to humankind, a complete system of faith and behavior, transmitted through God's final prophet, Muhammad and embodied in the Qur'an.

Central to Muslim belief is the concept of God as unique, infinite, all-powerful, and eternal—indeed, the Qur'an lists ninety-nine names for his attributes. He is at once immanent, pervading and sustaining the entire universe, and transcendent, not subject to the limitations of the material universe. He controls the life and death of all creatures, and is the measurer of all. Nature obeys him automatically, but human beings have free will, and here moral law replaces natural law. Humans have a choice; they should obey God, and if they do not, they will be punished.

The unity of God, *tawjid* (oneness), is always stressed. He is unique, and there are no other gods. To believe in other divinities is, for Muslims, the greatest sin, and is called *shirk*.

The five essential elements of Islam that one believes in are:
~ God
~ Angels
~ The revealed books
~ God's messengers
~ The Last Day

Supporting these are the Five Pillars of Islam:
~ Bear witness (*shahada*), a verbal profession of adherence to Islam: "There is no god but God, and Muhammad is his prophet." One must do this at least once in one's lifetime. Theologians make the distinction between *iman* (inner faith) and shahada, the latter naturally leading from the former.
~ One should pray five times each day at set times: before sunrise, early in the afternoon, late in the afternoon, immediately after sunset, and before retiring.
~ One must pay *zakah*, the religious tax, at least one-fortieth (2.5 percent) of one's wealth or income, which is intended for charitable causes.
~ During the month of Ramadan, the ninth month of the Muslim calendar, one must fast during daylight hours: no eating or drinking from dawn to dusk.
~ Make the Great Pilgrimage (*hajj*) to Mecca at least once in a lifetime, without affecting provision for one's family.

Below: the Sultan Ahmed Mosque, Istanbul, better known in the West as the Blue Mosque after the blue tiles originally on the interior walls. Built opposite the great Byzantine cathedral of Hagia Sophia, it dominated the skyline of the old city, with its 141-foot-high dome and six minarets.

Angels are believed to serve God in various functions. Created from light and without gender, they are messengers and also record the deeds of everyone in anticipation of the Last Day, when all will be judged. Some have specific roles, such as guarding and running hell and bearing God's throne. Israfil will be the one to sound a trumpet on the Last Day, summoning the dead to judgment. Greatest of the angels is Jibril (Gabriel), who passed the holy words of the Qur'an to Muhammad.

Heaven and Hell One's eventual fate is determined on the Last Day—the Day of Resurrection (*Yaum al-Qiyama*) will be followed immediately by the Day of Judgment (*Yaum al-Din*). All will then be judged by God. Muslims who have accepted the right belief, led good lives, and have repented their sins are destined for afterlife in heaven (*Janna*)—eternal bliss, allegorically described in such graphic terms as a beautiful garden with running waters, bounteous fruit, and pure maidens. Hell (*Jahannam*) is described as having seven levels, with fire, boiling pitch, and eternal torment, the lowest of the levels containing the tree of *Zaqqum*, the bad fruit of which sinners must eat.

None can intercede in God's judgment but Muhammad (although later traditions have added the names of other holy men). Those who do not accept Islam are termed *kafirs* (nonbelievers) and are doomed to eternal punishment in hell.

ISLAMIC WORSHIP

Above: *Ablutions before prayer* **Right:** *Performing rakah*

~ *Fatihah*: The opening sura of the Qur'an, which is thought to encapsulate the essence of the book.
~ Several verses from the Qur'an are recited.
~ *Rakah*: The worshipper carries out a series of movements with ritual chanting; these involve bending, prostration, and sitting.
~ *Shahada*: "There is no god but God, and Muhammad is his Prophet."
~ *Taslima*: Greeting neighbor worshippers by saying *Al-Salam alaykum* (Peace be upon you), which brings the prayer to an end.

Purpose-built mosques generally feature a dome and several minarets, tall towers atop which the muezzin (Arabic, *mua'zzin*, "the caller") traditionally calls the faithful to prayer. Men and women pray separately, sometimes the women behind the men, sometimes in a separate hall or simply segregated. In larger mosques there is often a great carpet in the hall with markings so that worshippers can take up their places in neat rows facing in the same direction. There is no altar.

The worshippers always pray facing in the direction of Mecca (this was originally Jerusalem, but was amended after the Prophet's migration, or *hijira*, to Medina). In the prayer room of the mosque, the *qibkla*, or direction of prayer, is indicated by a *mihrab* (niche) in the center of the appropriate wall.

Apart from this, the worship hall in a mosque is featureless, without any pictures—following the Islamic strictures on representation—and is instead decorated in the characteristic Islamic style with patterns, colors, and calligraphy.

The *Shari'a* embodies a code of worship, which can be individual or congregational. Muslims are required to pray (*salah*) five times each day. There are set times, which are posted at each mosque. Most important is the Friday prayer at noon, when the *imam*, leader of the prayers, will climb into the *minbar* (pulpit) and deliver a sermon in two parts to the faithful. (There is no hierarchical priesthood structure in Islam: imams are elected by the community.)

Entering a mosque, the worshipper removes his or her shoes. *Tahara* (purification) is required before worship, and most Muslims do this at home, but there are always facilities for ablutions at mosques. *Wudu* (minor ablutions) are appropriate to normal prayers, removing the impurifications of everyday life; *ghusl* (major ablutions) involve a complete body wash, such as are carried out to the dead before burial.

Prayers follow a set sequence, given below. One stands and faces the qibla.
~ *Niyyah*: The pronouncement of intention to pray.
~ *Takbi*: The Muslim confession of faith, *Allahu Akbar* (God is Great).

ISLAMIC FESTIVALS

The Hajj

The hajj is one of the Five Pillars of Islam, and believers must aspire to make this visit to Mecca at least once in their lifetime. It is carried out in the twelfth month of the Muslim calendar, Dhu al Hijjah, sometimes by millions of pilgrims. In recent times, the huge numbers of people have resulted in accidents and, tragically, considerable loss of life. Wearing simple, all-white clothing to symbolize purification, pilgrims follow a set pattern of events:

~ The *Ka'bah*, a cubic structure in the courtyard of the Great Mosque in Mecca, is circumambulated seven times in an counterclockwise direction.

~ *Sar'ee:* Pilgrims run seven times between the two low hills of Safa and Marwah. This is in memory of the efforts by Hagar, mother of Abraham's son, and Ishmael to find water in the desert when God showed them a stream.

~ At Mount Arafat (known as Mount Mercy, the place where God forgave Adam and Eve for their transgression in the Garden of Eden), pilgrims stand in meditation from midday to sunset.

~ They return to Mecca, pausing at Mazdalifa to gather pebbles.

~ Then at Mina they cast these pebbles at three pillars representing *Shaytan* (Satan), recalling Abraham's temptation and Satan's attempt to entice him away from God.

~ A sheep is ritually sacrificed, recalling God's testing of Abraham by commanding him to sacrifice his son, Ishmael.

~ *Eid ul-Adha* is the concluding feast, the Feast of the Slaughter. Some Muslims add *Hajji* (female, *Hajjah*) to their name after completing the Hajj.

This is the Great Pilgrimage; Muslims may make other, lesser pilgrimages (*umrah*) at different times of the year (and Shi'as make pilgrimages to particular tombs). The hajj is a very special occasion for a Muslim, often considered the greatest moment of their life. It is when Muslims meet others from different parts of the world and today the hajj also brings together political leaders of the Muslim world.

Sawm

Sawm, or fasting, is also of great importance and is observed in all Muslim countries, for fasting is another of the Five Pillars of Islam. It celebrates the month Ramadan (the ninth of the Islamic lunar year), in which the Qur'an was first revealed to humankind. Muslims do not eat, drink, smoke, or indulge in sex from dawn to dusk each day; they break their fast after sunset. In the night preceding the twenty-seventh day of Ramadan is *Laylat al-qadr*, the Night of Power, commemorating the descent by the angel Jibril and the beginning of revelations from God. It is the night when prayers are accepted and sins forgiven.

Eid Milad-un-Nabi

Celebrated on Rabee-ul-Awwal 12 of the Islamic year, this festival commemorates the birth of the Prophet; there is much feasting and speeches are made at the mosques recalling Muhammad's life and qualities.

Shab-e-Miraj

On Rajab 27, this festival commemorates the night of the Prophet Muhammad's miraculous ascent from Jerusalem to heaven, where he met Adam, Abraham, Moses, Jesus, and other prophets, and finally came "within two bow-shots" of God.

Ashura

Ashura, on the tenth day of Muharram, is a Shi'ite festival remembering the martyrdom of Husayn, the Prophet's grandson, and his family. There are ten days of mourning, during which the participants dress all in black; and on the tenth day there are

ISLAMIC SECTS

processions in which adherents scourge themselves to demonstrate the suffering of the martyrs.

Sunni Islam

Sunni Islam is no more than orthodox Islam, from which particular sects have broken away. The word *sunna* means "custom" or "code," especially in respect of the example of the Prophet, or Hadith. Its followers are thus thought of as "people of the sunna," hence Sunnis. They make up 85 percent of the world's Muslims and represent the traditional view of Islam.

Shi'a Islam

This is the second largest form of Islam, constituting some 15 percent of Muslims today. The term *Shi'a* refers to "partisans of Ali," who, according to the Shi'ites, was proclaimed successor to Muhammad by the Prophet himself after his last pilgrimage to Mecca and shortly before his death. Ali was of Muhammad's family, his cousin and adopted son as well as husband of the Prophet's daughter Fatima. Thus the descendants of Ali are recognized as the true leaders of Islam, or Imams. While an imam in orthodox Islam can simply refer to the leader of worship at a mosque, in Shi'a the term came to mean "rightful caliph," charismatic, divinely appointed, preserved from sin, acting with direct guidance from God, and able to deliver an inspired and infallible interpretation of the Qur'an. Being of the family of the Prophet, they are believed to possess insights (*jafr*) into the Qur'an passed to them by Muhammad himself. They alone can determine matters of doctrinal dispute.

Over the centuries, Shi'ism developed its own body of law, with relatively minor differences from that of the majority Sunnis. Today Shi'sm is important as the ruling sect in Iran, with substantial minorities in Iraq and the Indian subcontinent. The hostility between Sunni and Shi'a Muslims in Iraq after the deposition of Saddam Hussein in 2003 has escalated into a major sociopolitical issue.

Two principal branches of Shi'a Islam developed, each as a result of Imamic succession disputes.

Ismailis

The Ismailis (Seveners) emerged from a dispute concerning the succession of the Seventh Imam, who died before his father in the eighth century. Ismailis believe in seven rather than five pillars of faith: belief, purification, prayer, alms-giving, fasting, pilgrimage, and *jihad* (striving in the cause of God). Pilgrimage to the tombs of the Imams is believed to be especially meritorious, particularlt to Karbala (scene of the martyrdom of the Prophet's grandson Husayn) and Mashhad (tomb of the Eighth Imam). Ismailis also established the Fatimid dynasty in North Africa. Ismaili communities now constitute the second-largest of the Shi'a groups and survive in relatively moderate numbers in Syria, Iran, eastern Africa, and India, where their imams are titled "Aga Khan." The Forty-sixth Imam was granted the title by the Persian emperor and emigrated to India in 1840, settling in Bombay, where he was confirmed in his title by the ruling British.

The Nizaris are the principal Ismaili sect, currently number about 20 million and in

India are known as Khojas. Other subsects include:

The Qarmatians, who emerged during the ninth century as a secret, revolutionary sect and added elements of gnosticism to their creed. They established a utopian community in 899 and flourished in Iraq, Yemen, and Bahrain. They staged an uprising against the Abbasids about 900 and sacked Mecca during the hajj of 930, when they also abducted the Black Stone from the Ka'bah to Bahrain. It was returned twenty-two years later, and the Qarmatians faded away later in the eleventh century.

The Muqanna sect is the eponymous creation of a mid-eighth century Persian who was viewed as a heretic. He claimed to be an incarnation of God and led an insurrection, which the Abbasids extinguished in 779. His sect, however, continued into the twelfth century, and al-Muqanna's exploits inspired modern literature, including a short story by Jorge Luis Borges.

The Mutazilites began as a school of thought in Baghdad and Basra and flourished between the eighth and tenth centuries. They were the first to apply the methods of the Hellenic philosophers to Islamic doctrine. Among their dogmas was the concept of a created Qur'an, which became the official line under the Abbasids from 827 to 845.

The Assassins were a sect notorious in history for considering the murder of their enemies a religious duty. At the end of

Below: Pilgrims gather for the Ashura festival at the Mashad al-Husayn, shrine of the martyred third Shi'a Imam, Husayn, at Karbala.

the eleventh century, they established themselves in the hill fortress of Alamut and during the following century extended their activities across Persia, Iraq, and Syria with a network of strongholds. They gained their legendary image in the West by the picturesque report of Marco Polo of the use of hashish to produce a state of ecstasy and the promise of paradise for martyrdom while carrying out assassinations. Their reign of terror was ended by the capture of Alamut by the Mongols in 1256 and of Masyad (Syria) by Baybars in 1272.

Given the fact that Druzes permit neither conversion to nor from their religion and ban intermarriage, it is remarkable that they have survived into the twenty-first century. A secretive sect, they emerged in 1017 in Cairo, combining elements of Gnosticism, Neoplatonism, and transmigration. Their rites are closely guarded secrets. They believe that the Fatimid Sixth Caliph, whom they see as an incarnation of God, did not die, but vanished, and will one day return to begin a new golden age. Druze have been prominent, especially during recent troubles in Lebanon. Druze regard themselves as Muslims, but Muslims do not recognize them as such, and the Qur'an does not appear to feature in their creed.

Ithna Ashariyya

The Ithna Ashariyya (Twelvers) emerged with the disappearance of the Twelfth

Left: *The great Mosque at Djenné in Mali, built in 1906 and the largest clay building in the world. The walls are between 16 and 24 inches thick, necessary to support the tall structure. They also provide insulation from the heat of the day. The beams are of palm wood and are scaffolding for the annual replastering. The mosque and town were declared a UNESCO World Heritage Site in 1988.*

Imam in the tenth century; they constitute the majority of Shi'a Muslims and form the official religion of Iran today.

In Shi'ism, the Imams were chosen by family, descending from Ali and including his sons Hassan and Husayn. The Twelfth Imam, born in 869, succeeded upon the death of his father in 874 but remained secluded in *ghaiba* (meaning "absence" or "withdrawn by God"), answering questions indirectly—probably to protect him from the daggers of the Abbasids. In 939 it was announced that there would be no more Imams after this, but that the Imam would remain in "occultation" until called forth by God. Since then the "Hidden Imam" has given guidance and received prayer. He is

also referred to as *al-Mahdi* (the guided one), a term denoting a future, end-of-the-world figure who will reestablish peace and justice on earth before the end of days.

It was under the Saffavid dynasty (who claimed descent from the Seventh Imam), that Ithna Ashariyya was made the state religion of Iran. Pilgrimage to the tombs of the Imams is believed to be especially meritorious, most importantly to Karbala and Mashhad, as noted above.

Another sect is the Zaidis, or Fivers, who seceded over the succession of the Fifth Imam; for them, the Imamate is a matter of recognition rather than succession. They are closest to Sunnis and form the majority in Yemen.

SUFIS

Emotional and intuitive, Sufism is the mystic face of Islam, its followers not a particular separate sect, but rather a type of Muslim. As early as the first century of Islam, there emerged an ascetic, pietist aspect to the faith, seeking a return to the transcendental meaning of the Qur'an in reaction to the increasing legalism of the divine message.

The term *Sufism* has been sourced variously, perhaps from *tasawwuf* (self-purification) or from the simple woolen tunics (*sufi*) of ascetics, or from *Ahl-al-Suffa*—"the people of the bench"—constantly seen at prayer and study. While initially Muslims used the term *tasawuff*, *Sufism* has been the term used in the West since the early nineteenth century.

Sufis were concerned with the need for an inward-looking, devotional side to Islam. They turned away from worldly wealth, seeking purification of the heart and an inner, spiritual life leading to union with God, at the expense of human physical desires and needs. Through direct personal experience of God they hoped to arrive at the truth of divine love: reality (*haqiqah*) and intimacy with God, which, when attained, one becomes a saint, or *wali* (female, *waliyya*).

Sufi practices include a variety of mystical paths, with stages of attainment, often likened to a ladder with rungs (*maqam*) to ascend, characterized by:

~ Asceticism, few belongings, and regular fasting.
~ *Dhikr*, the recitation of the Ninety-Nine Beautiful Names of God or passages from the Qur'an.
~ Controlled breathing exercises and meditation.
~ Music and singing to express joy inexpressible by words.

Spiritual grace was deemed necessary, and a close relationship with a teacher (*shaykh*) was essential, since undisciplined

practices were seen as dangerous; therein lay other dangers, however, if the master were seen as infallible.

Spiritual purification is vital; following the *tariqah* (way or path) or science of self, one must remove all that is impure so that only the pure remains. The ascetic's ultimate goal is "annihilation" of the human self, with *zuhd* (detachment from the world), and *sabr* (patience), so that by destroying one's human attributes one acquired those of the divine, becoming as one with God. (An exemplar of this, with tragic consequences, was al-Hallaj, with his famous statement, "I am the Truth"—"Truth" being one of the names of God. He was executed for heresy.)

As time went on, some proponents of Sufis adopted more extreme practices, which were too exotic for the orthodox. The use of music, song, and dance could lead to hypnotic and ecstatic states (*hal* and *waja*), much frowned upon by the orthodox, especially when it was seen to degenerate into mere jugglery. Indeed, some later sects espoused more extravagantly extremist positions, including what was tantamount to pantheism. There were also political consequences of Sufism, which, in being antimaterialist, could also be anti-institutionalist because it posited the need for rulers to be spiritual and pious—thus implicitly criticizing authority. Early Sufis were at great pains to synthesize the internal and external aspects of Islam in order to avoid creating a distance between their positions and *Shari'ah* law, but some extreme sects were less careful about this. Sometimes Sufi sects were persecuted and forced underground. But Sufi orders have also been actively political—the Sanusiya order, for example, fought the colonial Italians, and the Tijaniya and Qadiryyas are still sociopolitically important in western Africa.

Missionary and educational work have been the Sufis' most important contributions to Islam. Sufis became the principal missionary elements, taking Islam to India, Turkey, central Asia, and sub-Saharan Africa. When orders began to settle in India early in the thirteenth century, their devotionalism and doctrines of equality attracted many Hindus. The spiritual education they undertook has also been of vast importance in the development and spread of Islam, and so too has their influence upon the arts. Arabic, Persian, Turkish, and Urdu literature has been enriched by Sufi influence, especially by mystical poetry.

Sufi sects include:

~ Qadiryyas, founded in the twelfth century in Iraq and now spread widely, from India to Morocco; trances are conjured up by dancing and music.

~ Dervishes (meaning "beggars") are famous, especially among tourists, in the form of *Mevlevis* (whirling dervishes) who induce trances by their spinning dances. Another sect, the Rifais, have been called "Howling Dervishes." When they reach a state of ecstasy by *dhikr*, they inflict pain on their bodies.

Other orders incude the Mevlevi, Naqshbandi, Shadhiliya, Tijaniya, the Ahmadiyya (or Badawiya after Sayyid Badawi of Tanta, Egypt), Sanusiya, Bektashiyya, and Chistiyah.

Above: *Sufis attaining ecstasy by dancing wildly to music. The movement is held to eliminate outward stimuli, leading to a trancelike state and mystical experience.*

Left: *The very modern Sabah State Mosque at Kota Kinbalu, Borneo, features a honeycomb-patterned dome.*

ABU HAMID MUHAMMAD AL-GHAZALI (1058–1111)

Abu Hamid Muhammad al-Ghazali was held in high esteem by his contemporaries—he has been considered the greatest religious authority after the Prophet and the most original thinker that Islam has produced. A professor of Islamic law and theology at Nizamiyah College, Baghdad, he experienced a spiritual crisis in 1095, in the sudden realization that while he taught about God, he did not know God. He embarked on a search for inner conviction, which led him to Sufism and the life of a mystic. Abandoning his brilliant teaching career, he traveled before establishing himself with disciples at Tus, in what was virtually a monastic community.

His attitude toward Sufism was moderate. Repudiating the excesses, including the worship of saints, he also disavowed any literal interpretation of the concept of "annihilation of the self" (see page 114) and the goal of becoming one with God as inconsistent with traditional Islamic theism. Instead, a careful observance of the duties set out by Islamic law could be the basis of a genuine Sufi life, but theology alone (the rational presentation of religious law, or *Fiqh*) was inferior to mystical experience.

His writings were very influential: *Ihya Ulum al-Din* (*The Revival of the Religious Sciences*) showed how Islam could be the basis of a profound devotional life, and *Tahafut al-Falasifah* (*The Incoherence of the Philosophers*) whipped up a storm among Islamic scholars and incited a spirited response from Ibn Rushd (known in the West as Averroes). His reputation spread far beyond Islam, and *The Incoherence of the Philosophers* was one of the first Arabic books to be translated into Latin, in the twelfth century.

Al-Ghazali's thinking led to a synthesis of Islamic theology and philosophy (including elements of Neoplatonism) and mysticism, producing a successful harmonization of Sufism with orthodoxy. This enriched Islam with a deeper inner dimension, and the result has characterized mainstream Sunni thought to the present day.

There was one negative aspect of his legacy, however: emphasizing the limits of the use of reason relative to faith was a factor in the withdrawal of Islamic scholarship from world leadership in science and philosophy.

BAHÁ'I FAITH

The Bahá'i Faith is a completely new world religion. It is not an Islamic sect, even though it originated in nineteenth-century Shi'ite Persia.

Sayyid 'Ali Muhammad, who called himself the Bab, meaning "the gate," proclaimed himself as a "Messenger of God," whose task was to prepare the way for a yet greater Messenger. This was seen as heresy by ruling Islam, and he was executed in 1850. His followers were known as Babists.

One Babist, Mirza Husayan 'Ali Nuri, took the name of Bahá'u'lláh (Glory of God), and in 1863 declared himself the New Messenger. He founded the Bahá'i Faith.

SCRIPTURES

The Bab wrote extensively, but it is not principally to his scriptures that the Bahá'i Faith looks—some of his laws have even been repealed by Bahá'u'lláh—but to the writings of Bahá'u'lláh and his successor as leader of the Bahá'is, Abdu'l-Baha. The most important of Baha'u'llah's approximately one hundred volumes, known as Tablets, are the *Kitab-i-Aqdas*: laws and social ordinances, and the *Kitab-i-Iqan*: theology.

Shoghi Effendi (1897–1957), Abdu'l-Baha's successor, translated many works into English and wrote interpretations of his predecessors' works. He also put in place an administrative system that he used to spread the Bahá'i Faith worldwide. The faith now has followers in every country in the world except the Vatican.

In 1963, following instructions in Bahá'u'lláh's writings, the Universal House of Justice was elected, and is now the authorized head of the faith. It can, if it wishes, legislate on matters not already covered by the scriptures. In general, however, the Universal House of Justice encourages Bahá'ists to make their own decisions on how to behave, based on spiritual and ethical precepts.

THE ESSENCE OF THE BAHÁ'I FAITH

The Bahá'i Faith's basic principles are the oneness of God, the oneness of religion, and the oneness of humanity. Thus all the religions of the world have emanated from the One God through different prophets, who include, but are not limited to, Krishna, Buddha, Muhammad, and Christ. Bahá'u'lláh is seen as the most recent prophet and so the most relevant, the one who has the message for today and whose religion is currently the evolutionary way forward for humanity. He is not, however, the final prophet.

The Bahá'i Faith teaches that all faiths contain the same ultimate spiritual truths even if they are expressed in different ways. Conflict derives not from man's spiritual laws but from their social laws. These were appropriate instruments of social cohesion in the past but have remained stagnant and are no longer relevant. The Bahá'i Faith sees worldwide change in social laws as the key to unity. The final step of evolution is

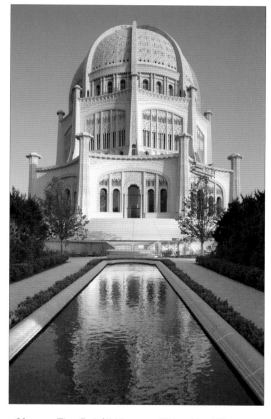

Above: *The Bahá'i House of Worship, Wilmette, near Evanston, North Shore, Chicago*

for all humanity to be one family in solidarity within which different cultures may flourish. Unity is not conformity; it is the removal of causes of conflict.

Some of the social tenets that will bring about this condition are:

Patriarchal societies esteem domination and power, which inevitably foster aggression, war, and greed—the balance needs to be redressed.

Education, which should primarily be concerned with values and morals and only secondarily with the acquisition of knowledge.

Elimination of sexual, racial, and class prejudice.

Elimination of extremes of wealth and poverty.

A world government with a global executive, because it is beyond the capacity of individual governments to deal with the crises that threaten the earth, notably pollution, global warming, and the control of multinational companies.

The efforts of today's governments to resolve the problems that beset humanity are bound to fail because they are based on the assumption that individual wealth and endless consumerism brings universal happiness. In accord with other faiths, the Bahá'i Faith teaches that true happiness and contentment come with detachment from wealth and from being of service to others.

INDIVIDUALS

The divine exists in everyone, and earth is a place of spiritual education where the soul may mature. However, salvation and the final oneness with God is a process. It started before birth and continues after death. And only the One God can judge where each individual stands on his or her own path.

Priests and religious leaders are forbidden in the Bahá'i Faith—it is up to the individual to discover the truth personally by reading the scriptures and reflecting on events in his or her own life. Marriage is seen as a bedrock for individual spiritual progress and each person should strive to act spiritually, bringing love, justice, and compassion to the world.

Individual spiritual rules include daily prayer, fasting, and refraining from alcohol and drugs.

WORSHIP

There are almost no rituals or public ceremonies in the Bahá'i Faith, and teachings specifically legislate against their development. There is one obligatory funeral prayer, and out of the many prayers that may be used in personal worship, there are three, one of which must be recited every day.

Every Bahá'i month the community gathers for the Nineteen-Day Feast, usually at someone's house. This has three aspects: devotional, where prayers and scriptures chosen by the host are read; administrative, where local issues are discussed; and social, which may include arts and other forms of culture.

HINDUISM

Hinduism can lay claim to being the world's oldest religion, dating back more than 5,000 years; but in fact it was not generally recognized as a specific, distinct religion until relatively recent times, and the word *Hindu* itself derives from a Persian word referring to the peoples of the Indus River region. Hinduism was not founded by any one person, nor can it be traced to one specific period in time. There is no ecclesiastical structure or centralized authority, no set creed, no single doctrine of salvation, no single sacred book. But, as diverse as it is, Hinduism nevertheless contains unifying strands and beliefs.

SACRED WRITING

Hindu literature comprises a vast body of work, the earliest being written in Sanskrit after having been passed down orally by sages (*rishi*) through the centuries. There are two principal categories of books:

Shrutis (literally, "heard," the word of God communicated to the sages), which contain the eternal principles of Hinduism and consist of the Vedas (knowledge), which describe the rituals, incantations, and hymns of ancient India. The basic text of each Veda is the *Samhita*, supplemented by later commentaries, including the *Brahmanas*, explaining ritual, and *Aranyakas* ("forest books," for hermits).

~ **Rig Veda** is the oldest text, and the others are based on it. It consists of a thousand hymns, organized in ten *mandalas*, or cycles, in praise of gods. It is the oldest book in any Indo-European language, having been written between 1500 and 1000 BCE.
~ **Sama Veda**, the Veda of chants, is intended as a text for the priest attending the *soma* sacrifice.
~ **Yajur Veda** sets out sacrificial prayers.
~ **Atharva Veda** is intended for private ritual and consists mainly of incantations and spells.

In addition, the Upanishads are works of philosophy and comment that explain the Vedas and include dialogues between gurus and students. They bring forth the idea of Brahman, the Universal Being, the World Soul.

Smritis (literally, "remembered") embody the practical application of the *Shrutis*, expounding social and moral codes, often allegorically in the form of myths and legends. The most famous, written by the great rishi Manu, explains the four stages of life and the caste system, while others, such as the *Niti Shastras* and *Kautilya Shastra*, provide advice for rulers. Within this body of literature are the eighteen *Puranas*, mythological stories, each emphasizing a theological position. The two most famous are the epics of the *Ramayana* and the *Mahabharata*, inspirational works that offer ideals to aspire to and give examples of nobility, kindness, faithfulness, and other such valued qualities. The *Ramayana* is the story of Rama as he rescues his wife Sita from the demon king, Ravana. The *Mahabharata* portrays a civil war between two branches of a ruling family and contains what is considered the jewel of Indian spiritual wisdom, the *Bhagavad Gita* (The Song of the Lord). This is in the form of a 700-verse poem spoken by Lord Krishna to his disciple, Prince Arjuna, on the battlefield of Kurukshetra before the climactic struggle between good and evil. He explains yogic and Vedic philosophies to provide a concise guide to self-realization and the nature of consciousness, the universe, and the Supreme. As such, it stands as the classic summary of the core beliefs of Hinduism.

Right: Hindus practice cremation (antyeshti), since the body is seen as merely a vehicle for the immortal soul. Adherents light a funeral pyre on the steps at the Hindu temple of Pashupatinath in Kathmandu.

Above: *A scene from a seventeenth-century wall painting in the Rajah's palace, Cochin, which illustrates scenes from the Ramayana. The central figure could be Ravana, the demon king who kidnaps Rama's wife Sita.*

YUGAS:
THE FOUR CYCLES OF THE WORLD
The Hindu cycle comprises a sequence of events—deterioration, destruction, return to chaos, rebirth—and the start of a new cycle. Each cycle is a day of Brahma equivalent to fourteen periods of *manu*. Each *manu* has four great ages, and each age has four *yugas*. Currently we are in the last—and worst—age, *Kaliyuga*.

PURUSHARTHA:
THE FOUR GOALS OF LIFE
Artha, worldly wealth and success but without greed. According to Kautilya (*c*. 300–400 BCE), "prosperity is the basis of a well-ordered state."
Kama, pleasure
Dharma, social and religious duty
Moksha, liberation

ASHRAMA: THE FOUR STAGES OF LIFE
In the long journey back to the Creator, human desires are fulfilled in four stages of life, from birth to death:

1. **Brahmacharya**, the student stage
2. **Grihasta**, "householder," the family life stage
3. **Vanaprastha**, "forest dweller," retirement with more devotion to spiritual activity
4. **Sanyasa**, preparation for *moksha*, during which one renounces all desires, possessions, and needs; one meditates all the time and ideally becomes a wandering holy man (*sanyasin*)

Within these stages are traditionally sixteen *Samskaras* (sacraments or ceremonies), of which four or five are regularly followed:
Jatakarma, the rituals surrounding birth
Namakarma, name-giving
Upanayana, confirmation of twice-born status for the three higher varnas, during the course of which the child is given a sacred thread and receives a mantra from his guru
Vivaha, marriage
Antyesti samskara, the funeral ceremonies

THE ESSENCE OF HINDUISM

Brahman is the name Hindus apply to the Absolute, thought of as a formless being everywhere, all knowing, all powerful, who transcends time and space. The self (*atman*) is identified with the Absolute and therefore with all things, so there is only one reality; all things are essentially part of each other.

There are three main schools of thought concerning Brahman, who can be regarded as *Nirguna Brahman* (without form/attributes) or *Saguna Brahman* (with physical qualities/attributes):

~ *Shankaracharya* in the *Advaita Vedanta* upholds the attributeless Brahman: there is only one Brahman; the individual soul is also Brahman, and therefore the material world is an illusion, or appearance (*maya*). This is absolute nondualism, expounded by Shankara (788–820).

~ *Ramanujacharya* in the *Vistavaita Vedandta* is attributed Brahman, who is without distinction; but individual selves and matter are real, though dependent on Brahman, being his instruments. This is therefore qualified nondualism, which was expounded by Ramanuja (1077–1157).

~ *Madhava charya* in the *Dvaita* school believes that the perfection of Brahman cannot be identified with the imperfect, created *atman*; there must be a fundamental distinction between man and God. Claims of unity threaten the transcendence of God. In this school there are five dualities, or distinctions: between God and the soul; between God and matter; between the individual soul and matter; between souls; and between individual components of matter. This is dualism, which was expounded by Madhva (*c.* 1197–1276).

The universe has no beginning or end, but comes forth from Brahman (the ultimate divine basis of being) and returns to Brahman in an endless cycle called *samsara*, which is connected by karma. The Upanishads make clear that supreme unity is self-realization, and in this alone are all differences harmonized. Time, causality, and the "micro–macrocosm" are all linked, so that one's actions (even the very smallest) affect the whole universe.

Creation is caused by the disturbance of balance between the three *gunas*, which are the three components of material nature (*prakrti*) present in all things except pure consciousness:

~ *Sattva*, luminosity, expressed in the individual as intelligence and virtue.

~ *Tamas*, darkness or heaviness, expressed in the individual as fear, stupidity, and sloth.

~ *Rajas*, force or movement, expressed in the individual as effort and activity, but also as wickedness and suffering.

Life is a long journey back to the Creator. It is interrupted by death, which leads to another body to continue the journey. The soul is born on earth many times in the samsara cycle, but endless rebirth entails suffering (*dukkha*). Samsara is the result of ignorance, so one has to replace this by knowledge. According to the law of karma, "as you sow, so shall you reap," and this is carried between incarnations.

A Hindu's aim is to escape samsara, the endless cycle, and to gain *moksha*—liberation, salvation, total freedom from pain and suffering. One must reach a state of mind to transcend the pain and pleasure of life to merge with the will of God; one thus attains moksha, freedom from the cycle of birth and rebirth and unification of the soul with Brahman. This is called yoga.

There are three paths (*margas*, or yogas) to moksha:

~ *Bhakti* (the way of devotion): worship Brahman through a particular image or form by constant prayer and loving devotion. The *Bhagavad Gita* says that all paths to salvation are equal, but this is seen as the highest path.

~ *Jnana* (the way of knowledge, wisdom): seek spiritual knowledge and enlightenment by study, meditation, and contemplation.

~ *Karma* (the path of action): by duty and good works. One should act with the mind fixed on Brahman, to become free and at peace. The results of one's actions are offered to Brahman to become one with him, and one hopes to progress through the castes.

MAYA In early Vedic teaching, *Maya* (illusion) is referred to as "supernatural power." In the Vedantas, it is the power of the supreme god to create the cosmic illusion of a differentiated universe that masks the reality of the actual divine unity. It creates ignorance of the individual self and realizes the evolution of the world by means of *sattva*, *rajas*, and *tamas*.

Left: *Mahabalipuram, the Dharmaraja-ratha, India*

THE HINDU PANTHEON

Hindu gods are often seen as one god in many guises. The many manifestations of God reflect different aspects of the Absolute and how he can be reached. Hindus generally adopt one of these gods, their *Ishtadeva* (chosen god) for worship—as Vishnu for Vaishnavas or Shiva for Shaivas, for example. Brahman, the Absolute, controls the universe by means of three major qualities. These qualities are known as the Trinity, or *Trimurti*, and are represented by the three principal Hindu gods: Brahma, the Creator; Vishnu, the Preserver; and Shiva, the Destroyer.

Vishnu and Shiva are inseparable and simultaneous. While Brahma is seen as the archetypal priest and Vishnu as the archetypal king, Shiva is regarded in the light of a yogi or renouncer.

Above: *The Trimurti—the Hindu trinity of Shiva, Vishnu, and Brahma—at the Temple of Shiva, Elephanta, India*

~ **Brahma** The light of the day and the dark of the night are his work; to create the world and humans he made a goddess out of himself, half woman (*Gayatri, Saraswati*) and half man. He is depicted with four heads, from which the four Vedas are said to have come.

~ **Vishnu** The preserver and protector has qualities of mercy and goodness. When the balance between good and evil turns in favor of demons, Vishnu is incarnated in a human form to restore the balance—to destroy evil and restore right. Vishnu is worshipped mainly in his incarnations as Rama and Krishna and is often represented lying on the coiled serpent, Shesha, with Lakshmi massaging his feet; he is shown with conch, disk (*vaaijra*), club, and lotus (*padma*). Ten of these incarnations, or avatars (not all human), are generally recognized:

1 **Matsya**: Fish
2 **Kurma**: Turtle, symbol of perseverance. At the Churning of the Oceans (see page 32), his carapace served as the base of Mount Mandora, enabling the rescue of many precious things lost in the flood.
3 **Varaha**: Boar
4 **Narasingha**: Lion
5 **Vamana**: Born as a dwarf, he achieved the restoration of the world to the gods by tricking the demon king Bali.
6 **Parasurama**
7 **Rama**: The central figure of the *Ramayana*, in which he defeats the demon king Ravana in single combat after a great battle. He is seen as the ideal of manhood and a role model for humanity. He is depicted colored blue and holding a bow and arrow.
8 **Krishna**: The embodiment of love and divine joy, protector of sacred utterances and—since he grew up as a cowherd—cows. A trickster and lover, he is famed for his adventures as a boy, when he played the flute. He is the deity of humor. Hero of the *Mahabharata* in the *Baghavad Gita*, he speaks on the essence of *bhakti yoga*. In southern India he is known as Mayon.
9 **Buddha**: See pages 124–27.
10 **Kalki**: Will come at the end of the *Kaliyuga*, the present period of decline, and will appear on a white horse.

~ **Shiva** Associated with generation and destruction, Shiva is the destroyer of the world and god of yogis. He receives devotion as a *bhakti* god, and Shaivas paint their faces with three horizontal lines symbolizing the triple aspect of Shiva: creator, destroyer, and preserver. As a personal god, Shiva can be worshipped as Nataraja, Lord of the Dance (symbolic of the cosmic dance of creation and destruction, the turning of the wheel of life), and is portrayed as a dancer from the fifth century. He can also be seen as Daksinamurti, a spiritual teacher. Worshippers are often ascetics, and smear their bodies with ashes. Shiva is portrayed with three eyes (the third, vertical in the center of the forehead, is the eye of wisdom), with the ascetic's piled-up hair in which sit the crescent moon and often Ganga, as the Ganges is said to flow through his hair. Skulls and snakes—showing that he is beyond the power of death—and the narcotic flower *datura* are his ornaments, and a trident, representing the three gunas (replaced in southern India by an axe). He rides a white bull named Nandi (meaning "joyful"), or is often seated on a tiger skin, representing the mind. In unborn form, Shiva is represented by the phallic *lingam* (male creative energy), accompanied by the *yoni* (the female principle); in early representations dated to about 600, Shiva is shown with an erect phallus.

Above: *In a seventeenth century parchment from Rajasthan, Vishnu rests between the destruction of the world and the creation of the new universe. He sleeps on the serpent Ananta, who represents eternity. With him is Lakshmi, and at the top left Vishnu rides the Garuda.*

GODS

~ **Balarama** Brother of Krishna; symbol of strength, duty, and honesty. He killed the demon Dhenuka. His wife is Revati, Raivata's daughter.

~ **Dhanwantri** Physician of the gods, and to some an incarnation of Vishnu. It was he who emerged from the Churning of the Oceans (see page 32) bearing the chalice containing *amita*, the draught of immortality.

~ **Ganesha** "Lord of Hosts," the elephant-headed brother of Kartikaya, and son of Shiva and Parvati. He rides a rat, a symbol of the defeated demon of vanity, and has a broken tusk, part having been removed to write the *Mahabharata*. He is god of luck, learning, and wisdom and one of the best-loved of the gods. He is invoked before all undertakings because of his ability to create the faith that removes all obstacles. He is often depicted with four hands: one in the act of blessing, one holding a rosary, one holding a snake (which is identified with control over death), and the fourth holding his broken tusk.

~ **Garuda** King of the birds, seen as the messenger between gods and men. He is depicted as a crowned bird or as a bird with a human head.

~ **Hanuman** The monkey god, famed for courage, strength, and selfless service; also considered to manifest the supposed monkeylike qualities of mischief and humor. A major character in the *Ramayana*, he led a band of monkeys to help Rama rescue his wife, Sita, from Ravana. He is the patron of wrestlers and bodybuilders and is also seen as representing the relationship of a servant to his master.

~ **Kartikaya** Son of Shiva and Parvati, brother of Ganesha; the scientist of the gods. He is also god of war and pestilence, and otherwise known as Skanda, Kumara, or Murugan. He slew the demon (*asura*) Taraka and is shown riding on a peacock, holding a spear; he is often depicted with six heads and twelve hands.

Left: The rich panoply of a Hindu temple roof in Singapore

Right: Ganesha, his foot resting on his vahana (vehicle), a rat

Above right: Kartikaya with his vahana, a peacock

Far right: Hanuman, the monkey god

HINDU GODDESSES

Female deities are manifestations of Devi, the Divine Mother, the Great Goddess, and are worshipped equal to or as consorts of male gods. Their overriding quality is compassion and benignity (as Lakshmi and Sri, for example), but some incarnations are formidable (as Durga and Kali). In Vedic times, Devi was the Goddess, manifestation of natural forces, as Ganga (the river Ganges), Ratri (the night), and Usas (the dawn). Later these were drawn together as the Great Goddess, Mahadevi, the source of all energy in the cosmos. Her main forms are as Durga, Parvati, and Kali, but there are many others. Shaktas believe that Devi is in fact the ultimate source of all, and that the other gods are merely her agents.

~ **Annapurna** Household goddess, incarnation of Parvati symbolizing divine nourishing care; images are found in Hindu kitchens.

~ **Bhudevi** Earth goddess, seen in southern India, particularly as the second most important of Vishnu's wives, having been linked with him in the Puranas. In the Vedas she is coworshipped with Dyaus, the sky god.

~ **Bhuvaneshwari** The queen of the phenomenal world.

~ **Dhumavati** The eternal widow, an ugly form of Shakti, the creative power in Hinduism. She was the Divine Mother at time of the deluge. Her flag bears images of a black crow, the symbol of black magic.

~ **Durga** Another aspect of Kali, and is beautiful in contrast to Kali's dark, ugly appearance. To kill the demon Mahish (and again, when evil threatens the balance of the world), all the gods contribute a quality to her weaponry, making her one formidable divine force. She is portrayed with a third eye, has ten arms (sometimes eighteen) and rides a lion or tiger. She is supported by ten *yogini* (demonesses), who follow up her victory over evil.

~ **Ganga** Sister of Parvati, the incarnation of the river Ganges, flowing from the foot of Vishnu through the matted hair of Shiva. She is often depicted resting in Shiva's hair in river or goddess form.

Above: Images of gods adorn a Hindu temple in Singapore.

~ **Kali** The ferocious incarnation of Devi. She represents the realities of time and death—the frightening aspects of life. Her appearance is terrifying, her skin black or dark blue, and she is garlanded with human skulls.

~ **Lakshmi** Goddess of light, beauty, good luck, and wealth, symbolizing love and grace. All the gods fell in love with her, but she was given to Vishnu and appears as his consort at each of his reincarnations. She is commonly portrayed dressed in red and surrounded by lotuses (as the beautiful flower grows in mud, so does humanity flourish in this harsh world). Gaja-Lakshmi is an ancient depiction of her being bathed by elephants, symbolic of the clouds of the rainy season. Her image is often seen on doorposts, to ward off evil.

~ **Matangi** The Dark One, a form of *Saraswati* who resides in the throat chakra. She is invoked to achieve command over speech, knowledge, and creativity.

~ **Parvati** Consort of Shiva, mother of Ganesh and Kartikay. With Shiva she is worshipped in a beautiful form, holding a lotus. Worshipped alone she can be Durga or Kali, destroying evil and protecting the good. She rides a tiger and is depicted with eight hands, in which she holds the symbols of her power.

~ **Saraswati** Consort of Brahma, goddess of knowledge and the creative arts. She is also Vac Devi, goddess of speech. Dressed in white (symbolizing purity of motive in the search for knowledge), she rides a swan or peacock while playing music on a veena. She holds a rosary (*mala*) and a palm-leaf scroll, symbolizing knowledge.

~ **Shakti** Consort of Shiva, she is worshipped in many guises, including those of Durga, Kali, and Amba. Shakti also refers generally to the female aspect of deity, complementing the male, and assumes a creative role resembling Maya.

~ **Sita** Great heroine of the *Ramayana*.

VAHANAS (vehicles) are the means by which the gods are conveyed and are also the animal symbols of the gods, icons linked to the god's attributes.							
Agni	ram	Ganesh	rat	Indra	elephant	Saraswsati	swan/peacock
Bhairava	dog	Ganga	makara, a mythical crocodile-like creature	Kama	parrot	Shiva	bull
Bhudevi	elephant			Kartikay	peacock	Varuna	fish
Brahma	swan			Lakshmi	elephant	Yama	buffalo
Durga	lion/tiger	Garuda	bird	Parvati	lion/tiger	Yamuna	turtle

HINDU WORSHIP

Hindus are free to worship the deity of their choice (their *ishtadeva*). For example, Shaktas worship the Divine Mother, Devi, or Maha; Shaivas worship Shiva; and Vaishnavas worship Vishnu (usually as Lord Krishna). While they are worshipped as distinct gods, they are at the same time forms of Brahman, the one ultimate reality. Most temples (*mandir*) in India are dedicated to a single deity, which is at the same time a symbol of the whole; outside India there has been an evolution toward temples embracing all deities. Images (*murti*) of deities in temples are regarded as living, so they are washed, offered food, put to sleep, and so on; the power (*shakti*) of the god is actually present.

Because worship (*puja*) is an individual rather than collective act for Hindus, most Hindus also have a shrine in their homes with a picture of the god, decorated with flowers, incense, and colored powders.

Hindus will perform several acts of purification before approaching the deity or entering a temple. They touch the floor upon entering and remove their shoes. A bell is rung to alert the devotee into realizing he or she is in the presence of God, and incense is burned. The worshipper stands, hands folded, facing the shrine to pray, or prostrates himself. He or she may then offer fruits, flowers, milk, or money to the god before circumnavigating the shrine clockwise—for, as the earth goes around the sun, God is at the center of life.

The *Arti* ceremony, the offering of light, is performed two or three times a day. The priest lights five lamps in the *arti* plate (cotton wicks in clarified butter); he rotates the *arti* clockwise before each deity, then passes each hand over the light to the forehead, receiving the light of God. Offered food is collected and distributed among devotees as *prasad* (blessed food). In addition, a *diya* (a small sacred lamp) is lit in the morning or at twilight.

THE CASTE SYSTEM

The word *caste* is of Portuguese origin and relates to two similar but not strictly identical concepts: *varnas* (from color) and *jatis* (from race). The former date from Vedic times in northern India and, according to the *Rig Veda*, the four classes were constituted at the creation of the world; *jatis* reflect the social divisions and subdivisions in Indian communities today and run into the thousands. The latter stem from the former and have long been the object of reformers in the subcontinent. The four castes are:

~ **Brahmins** are spiritual guides, the learned; priests.
~ **Kshatriyas** are protectors of society; the lawmakers, warriors, and rulers.
~ **Vaishyas** are providers of food and sustenance; farmers, merchants, and commoners.
~ **Sudras** are servers of the community; servants and artisans.

Karma determines the caste into which one is born, and there are rules of conduct (*Varnasaramadharma*) appropriate to each, covering kinship, behavior, diet, occupation, and much else. Traditionally the first two castes have shared spiritual and temporal power, united in contradistinction to the others, and the first three classes are seen as twice-born (*dvija*); they wear a sacred thread looped over the left shoulder, hanging to the right hip. Outside and below this system are the Untouchables, the lowest social order. They were called *harijans* (children of God) by Gandhi; but they themselves prefer the word *dalit* (oppressed).

HINDU FESTIVALS

During the many Hindu festivals, temples fill with worshippers, revealing the vibrancy of Hindu life. Some of the most important festivals are:

~ **Diwali** (or *Deepavali*) lasts for five days, the fourth of which is Hindu New Year's Day. It takes place in October and November and is known as the Festival of Light. Candles and lamps are placed in windows to welcome Rama home to his kingdom as rightful king.
~ **Navaratri**, "Nine Nights," is dedicated to the Divine Mother.
~ **Janmashtami**, during July or August, celebrates the birth of Lord Krishna.
~ **Holi** is in February or March, the start of the spring or hot season in India. A joyful festival, it is dedicated to Krishna. Hindus throw colored water and powders at each other, without barriers of rank or caste, and visit friends in the evening.
~ **Dussehra**, in September or October, celebrates the triumph of good over evil and often involves acting out the *Ramayana* story, the victory of Rama over Ravana. It includes *Navaratri* (the Festival of Nine Nights), culminating in celebrations for *Durga*.
~ **Ganesha**, August to September.
~ **Shivartri**, dedicated to Shiva, is in January or February.

In addition, there are many localized festivals, such as **Kumbha-Mela**, held every three years at the four different locations—Hardwar, Nasik, Prayaga, and Ujjain—where drops of amrita, the nectar of immortality, fell.

Right: *Taking to the waters of the Ganges at Kumba-Mela. These festivals are some of the biggest religious celebrations in the world, attracting millions of adherents. Concern about pollution in the waters provoked protest in 2007.*

BUDDHISM

Buddhism grew as part of the Shamana tradition, which is older than Hinduism. It shares reincarnation and karma, the law of cause and effect, as major tenets. The essential break with Hinduism was the central belief in gods, although the Buddha does not deny the existence of God or supernatural beings. He rejects the caste system and sacrificial cults.

There have been three types of Buddhism:

~ Sravaka, of which only Theravada survives
~ Mahayana
~ Vajrayana, "the Diamond Way," to reach Buddhahood in this lifetime, via mantras

Buddhism spread to Central and Southeast Asia, Japan, China, and Korea. Theravada spread south in the third century BCE, by the time of the Mauryan Emperor Asoka reaching present-day Sri Lanka; then to Thailand and the remainder of Southeast Asia. Emperor Asoka sent Buddhist missionaries to Sri Lanka, the area of the Himalayas, to Burma, Afghanistan, even to Egypt, Macedonia, and Cyrene. King Menander, or Milinda (160–145 BCE), an Indo-Greek ruler whose kingdom centered in present-day Pakistan, is said to have converted to Buddhism; his coins bear the eight-spoked dharma wheel.

During the first century CE, Buddhism reached China, where it complemented parts of Taoism but was opposed at first by Confucianism; it took root, however, and Zen originated in China.

In India, however, Buddhism was in decline by the twelfth century and gradually assimilated into Hinduism, virtually disappearing as a separate religion.

The Councils

Shortly after the death of the Buddha, a council was held by 500 *arahats* (enlightened monks) at Rajagriha to agree on a definitive version of the Buddha's teaching, as yet passed on only orally. The *Tripitaka*, the Scriptures, resulted, and 227 rules were laid down. Further councils refined the doctrines and led to the split between Theravada and Mahayana Buddhism. The council at Patna in 244 BCE was called by Emperor Asoka and succeeded in completing the Tripitaka. At a council called by Kanishka, king of a Kashmir-based kingdom, three commentaries emerged, which became the basis for the Tibetan scriptures.

Above: *Household shrines for sale in a Thai shop*

Left: *The Sukhothai Traimit Golden Buddha at the Traimitwitthayaram Temple, Bangkok. Made of pure gold, it is the largest golden Buddha in the world. It is 700 years old, and for centuries was covered with plaster to conceal it from invaders; only in 1931 was the golden image revealed beneath its covering.*

THE SACRED WRITINGS

The sermons and teachings of the Buddha were not written down for many years. The complete surviving canon of scripture is in Pali (an ancient Indian language), the first written scriptures we know of, and were set down in present-day Sri Lanka during the first century BCE. The Sacred Writings, or Tripitaka, were gathered at the councils to form the Pali Canon, outlining the central doctrines of Buddhism.

The Tripitaka (Sanskrit), or Tipitaka (Pali), consists of three *Pitakas* (baskets):
~ *Vinaya*—rules for monks (*bhikkhus*) and nuns (*bhikkhunis*)
~ *Sutta*—the Buddha's sermons
~ *Abhidhamma*—commentary, philosophical analysis of the Buddha's teachings

Right: *A guardian of the Emerald Buddha in the Royal Monastery in Bangkok. The Emerald Buddha is actually carved from a block of green jade and was discovered in 1434 in a shrine at Chiang Rai.*

Buddhists take refuge in
The Three Jewels
~ The Buddha
~ Dharma
~ The *Sangha*

The Five Precepts
~ Respect life: do not kill or harm
~ Do not steal
~ No sexual misconduct
~ No lies or slander
~ No intoxicating substances

Left: *Chinese-style Buddha in a Singapore temple*

THE ESSENCE OF BUDDHISM

The essential insight of the Buddha is the perception of the interdependence and impermanence of all things. All beings suffer (*dukkha*), the cause of which is selfish desire and a lack of understanding of the nature of the self.

The self is a collection of aggregates (*skandhas*) constantly in flux, consisting of five elements:
~ Form (bodily events)
~ Feelings
~ Perception
~ Mind-contents (disposition)
~ Consciousness
The relationship between these determines the self at any given time. It also creates karma (action and reaction), and karma influences birth, life, and rebirth—which will not necessarily be in human form. The skandhas are dispersed at death and reassembled upon rebirth.

To escape suffering, one must address the Four Noble Truths and the Noble Eightfold Path. One acquires merit in successive lives by following the Buddha's rules, the sooner to reach nirvana. Then one loses individuality "as the dewdrop slips into the shining sea," merging with the universal life.

The essence of Buddhism, therefore, is to:
~ Seek dharma.
~ Achieve nirvana (not by divine intervention but by personal effort).
~ Attain freedom from *samsara* (endless birth and rebirth).

The Four Noble Truths
~ Suffering is the result of karma.
~ *Samudaya*: The cause of suffering; craving (*tanha*), or desire.
~ *Nirodha*: There is an escape from suffering, to eliminate craving, and attain freedom from recurring delusion (samsara).
~ *Magga*: The way to escape from suffering is to follow the Noble Eightfold Path to nirvana.

The Noble Eightfold Path
The Noble Eightfold Path is represented by the dharma wheel and is also known as the Middle Way toward a skillful, balanced, practical lifestyle. It consists essentially of truth, insight, and serenity; ethical conduct; and spiritual discipline, devoted to:

Pragya (wisdom):
~ Right view, understanding, attitude
~ Right aim, intention, resolve, motive, thought

Shila (virtue):
~ Right speech; no lies, slander, or gossip
~ Right action, conduct
~ Right livelihood, means of living without doing harm to others

Samadhi:
~ Right effort
~ Right mindfulness, awareness of things as they are
~ Right concentration, contemplation, meditation

Dharma
Dharma is the Buddha's insight and teachings, and includes nirvana, karma, and reincarnation. Nirvana is actually not explained by the Buddha; essentially it is beyond words. It means relief from the pain and misery of the world, an ineffable, transcendental state.

Karma is deeds or feelings and binds all people to the cycle of birth and rebirth. This is the law of moral causation: all actions have a consequence in this and the next life. Reincarnation reflects actions in the previous life or lives, which leads to dukkha. To achieve nirvana and escape dukkha, one must practice meditation and austerity.

THERAVADA

Adherents of Theravada (The Way of the Elders) believe they practice the original form of Buddhism, based upon the Four Noble Truths, the Eightfold Path, the Five Precepts, and the Tripitaka, or the Pali Scriptures conservatively interpreted. Prime importance is given to the Sangha and individual liberation. It is practiced in Sri Lanka, Thailand, and Burma.

Monastic life is central, and the goal is to attain rebirth in a life where one can become a monk or nun, and thus work toward nirvana. The Sangha, which claims unbroken succession from the Buddha, is supported by lay charity; monks are not allowed to work or have money; their possessions are their robes, personal items, and a begging-bowl.

There are ceremonies, but worship in temples consists of *puja*, recitation of parts of the Pali Scriptures, and chanting to mark important times in life. Meditation is also important and includes the following:

~ *Samatha*: concentration
~ *Mindfulness*: awareness of the activities of the body and mind
~ *Metta*: loving kindness
~ *Vipassana*: insight, awareness of the ever-changing self

THE SANGHA

Sangha, or monasteries, consist of *Arahats* (worthy ones, or saints) enlightened by the Buddha's teaching. To become a Buddhist monk or nun, one must receive a formal ordination and leave one's family, relying on charity to survive.

Monks ordain others and spread the message of dharma. Monks and nuns are celibate, and the nuns are subservient to monks. Monks are said to need three robes, all saffron-colored, including a *dhoti* (a long cloth worn around the waist) and a shawl to wear around the shoulders. Sometimes monks are hermits and sometimes they live a communal life.

MAHAYANA

This school of Buddhism results from the tension between the inward-looking nature of Theravada and the need for consideration for others. In Mahayana, the intention is to seek enlightenment for all beings instead of just the individual. This new Buddhism was called Mahayana, meaning "the Greater Vehicle." (Mahayana Buddhists referred to Theravada deprecatingly as "the Lesser Vehicle," or *Hinayana*.)

The Mahayana Scriptures, central to this tradition, are claimed to be the last teachings of the Buddha and include the ***Perfection of Wisdom*** suttas, the famous ***Lotus Sutra***, and the ***Nirvana Sutra***. Many have been translated into Tibetan and Chinese. (Theravadans regard them as deviant works, not originating from the Buddha.) There are also subsequent additions to the scriptures, some seen as spurious, some new.

Bodhisattvas—"Beings of Wisdom" or "Buddhas-in-waiting"—work toward personal nirvana but also do good to others. Often spiritualized beings and disciples of the Buddha, they have delayed their own enlightenment until all beings are free of suffering; their help can be invoked by Buddhist worshippers.

The austere monastic style of Theravada is replaced by *bhakti* (warm devotion). To achieve merit on the path to enlightenment, worship (*puja*) is practiced—and thus there are more statues and shrines in this branch of Buddhism—while nirvana can also be reached by outward actions in addition to internal means.

"Buddha Nature" posits that Buddhahood is not limited to the ordained but is the real nature of living beings, already within the individual, awaiting revelation, which can be helped by teaching.

Mahayana Buddhism has spread to Tibet, China, Vietnam, Korea, and Japan.

Below: Worship at a typical Buddhist shrine in Thailand, atop the Golden Mount (Wat Sraket), Bangkok

MANTRAS
are sacred chants performed while meditating. The most famous is:
"Om Mani Padme Hum," which means "Jewel in the Lotus." The first and last words are resonant sounds of spiritual significance.

ZEN

Zen, meaning "meditation," originated in sixth-century China and spread to Japan, where it developed into several distinct forms. In essence, it holds that the Buddha's message is beyond words. The Buddha's Silent Sermon, or the Flower Sermon, illustrates this. The Buddha held a lotus before his disciples; alone of them, Kasyapa (Maha Kasyapa) smiled, whereupon the Buddha gave him the lotus, saying, "What can be said I have said to you. What cannot be said I have given to Kasyapa." The tradition was passed to Bodhidharma, founder of Zen Buddhism in China, who traveled there in 530 CE. Zen spread to Japan, Korea, and Vietnam, and in the twentieth century Zen was brought to the West, where it became fashionable.

JAPANESE ZEN

~ **Rinzai Zen**, founded by Eisai (1141–1215), uses meditation (*za-zen*) based on riddles (*koans*, problems requiring great mental concentration) to which there are no logical answers. The confusion caused by these koans result in a "great ball of doubt," altering one's way of thinking. When this doubt is shattered, enlightenment comes. This thought process demonstrates the power of intuition over reason. It was much favored by the samurai, but declined toward the end of the seventeenth century.
~ **Soto Zen**, founded by Dogen (1200–53), was the second school, emphasizing sitting meditation, during which enlightenment was gradually revealed.
~ **Obaku Zen**, the smallest branch, was founded in China, with Chinese traditions that include chanting, ceremonies, and Pure Land teaching.

Zen has had a specific impact upon the arts—everything from calligraphy, painting, and the tea ceremony to flower-arranging and music. Calligraphy, in particular, often replaces the Buddha image in shrines.

TIBETAN BUDDHISM

This developed in isolation from mainstream Buddhism as a result of the area's location and consists of several schools of thought.

Lam Rim (the graduated path) is the principal teaching.
Stage 1:
~ Refuge in the Triple Jewel of Buddha, Dharma, and Sangha
~ Ethical behavior
~ Basic meditation
Stage 2: Meditation to overcome greed, anger, and ignorance, and understanding the interdependence of all living beings
Stage 3: The Bodhisattva Path, seeking full enlightenment for all beings via development of Great Compassion and Perfect Wisdom—particularly compassion

Vajrayana is the highest practice, the aim of which is to reach Buddhahood in this current lifetime. Gurus, or *lamas*, act as guides to the gods, spirits, rituals, and mantras that lead to nirvana. Vajrayana spread from India to Nepal and later to Tibet, China, and Japan. It contains elements of Tantrism (an ancient Indian ritual) and of Bön (the shamanistic folk religion of Tibet). Vajrayana's aim is to realize the Absolute by means of mantra and ritual; in effect, it is a mixture of Mahayana, mystical Tantric Buddhism, and Bön.

THE DALAI LAMA
The Dalai Lama is the spiritual head of Tibetan Buddhism. Each Dalai Lama is believed to be the reincarnation of the bodhisattva Avalokiteshvara; when one dies, the next appears as a child, who undergoes rigorous investigation to assure his identity. The current Dalai Lama is the fourteenth and was forced into exile in 1959 by the Chinese to Dharmasala in India. He has been Dalai Lama since 1940 and won the Nobel Peace Prize in 1989.
Left: *With U.S. president George W. Bush at the White House, May 2001*

BUDDHIST FESTIVALS AND HOLY DAYS

These are generally joyous occasions and include the celebration of significant days in the life of the Buddha as well as birthdays of bodhisattvas. They vary according to tradition and country. Theravada celebrations generally include *paritta*, chanting to combat negative spirits. The lunar calendar is used to calculate the dates for holy days, but in the Zen tradition there are fixed dates—February 15, *Parinirvana*; April 8, the Buddha's Birthday; October 3, Bodhidharma Day; and December 8, the Buddha's Enlightenment.

Amitabha (the Buddha of Infinite Light) is important in the Pure Land tradition.
Asalhapuja, or **Dharmacakra**, celebrates the Buddha's First Sermon.
Avalokitesvara's Birthday (Kuan Yin).
Hana Matsuri, the Buddha's birthday in the Zen tradition, in April.
Higan, the spring and autumn equinoxes, in Japan.
Kandy Perahara, a ten-day festival in the old Sri Lankan capital, when the sacred tooth relic of the Buddha is paraded.
Kathina, a monastic festival celebrated in Thailand and involving the Thai royal family.
Maghapuja, or All Saints' Day.
Mahayana Mahaparinivana, the Buddha's death; observed throughout the Buddhist world.
Pavarana (Sangha Day) ends the Rains Retreat in Southeast Asia.
Poson celebrates the coming of Buddhism to Sri Lanka; full moon of June.
Ulambana (Ancestor Day), when the gates of hell open and ghosts visit the world for fifteen days.
Uposatha observance days (Theravada) involve renewed dedication to the dharma.
Vesak, or **Vaisakhapuja**, is the most important of festivals and falls on the full moon in May; it celebrates the birth, enlightenment, and death of the Buddha.

JAINISM

In terms of numbers of adherents, Jainism does not rate as one of the great world religions, but in fact Jain influence on Indian philosophy, and thought, as well as religious, social, and economic life, has been out of all proportion to numbers. Evolving over the centuries, Jainism is an ethical doctrine with self-discipline at its heart, a faith of the utmost rigor. It is also a very tolerant religion, believing that, since all beings can attain divinity, there is no conflict between man's duty to himself and to society.

JAIN SCRIPTURE

There is no single Jain bible; texts have been written throughout the centuries of Jain history and added to the canon. Such writings can be deemed sacred, even those of relatively recent composition. The ancient scriptures have oral beginnings, as monks and nuns were not allowed to possess books (a restriction that has since been reversed). There are essentially three groups of scripture: the Purvas (meaning "previous"), composed of lost scripture, accepted as authoritative by both major sects; *The Twelve-Limbed Basket* (the twelfth is lost); and five groups of additional texts by later ascetic teachers. The two main sects of Jainism, Shvetambara and Digambara, disagree on the validity of the latter two.

There is an inherent impermanence to oral traditions, however—the Jains are said to have discovered this in 350 BCE when a famine killed many monks, many memorized texts were lost. Both the main sects agree that the Purvas were lost at this time; the names of the texts survived but not the contents (if, inded, they ever did exist). Regardless, the Purvas were accepted as the basis of Jain tradition. Thereafter, a series of conferences and assemblies attempted to preserve oral teachings in a more systematic and permanent way.

Above: *A votive painting depicting an unnamed Tirthankara seated on an elaborate throne*

The Twelve-Limbed Basket

The Twelve-Limbed Basket, or *Angas*, consists of each of Mahavira's disciples' oral versions of his teachings. The Shvetambara claimed their scriptures came directly from *The Twelve-Limbed Basket*. The Digambara claim that *The Twelve-Limbed Basket* was lost by the second century, so the spilt between the two sects is largely a question of authority. Both scriptural traditions have the same roots, however. The Shvetambara identify the *upanagas* (supplementary texts), some 22 *sutras*, to be associated with the *Twelve Angas*.

The Shvetambara Canon

This body of work is said to have been fixed at three councils that collected this material, turning oral accounts into written text; representatives of the Digambara sect were not present and do not accept the outcome. The first council, at Patna 160 years after the death of Mahavira, is the first official canon; simultaneous meetings at Mathura and Valabhi 827 years after Mahavira's death resulted in some inevitable discrepancies. The final assembly was at Valabhi in 453 or 466 CE, but no written list exists of what was

agreed. Not all Shvetambara accept all these texts as authoritative; in particular, the Sthanakvasi and Terapanthi branches reject texts that support image worship.

The Kalpa Sutra (*The Book of Ritual*) perhaps dates in part from the second century BCE and contains a biography of Mahavira, together with regulations (*kalpa*) for the behavior of monks. This is one of the two principal texts of the Shvetambara sect and contains the earliest known account of Mahavira's life. It is written in the language of Ardhamagadhi and is recited during the festival of Paryushan.

Tattvarthasutra

This sets out the path of spiritual progress in fourteen stages (see opposite) and is accepted by both major sects. It was written in the fourth or fifth century by Umasvati. The first significant text in Sanskrit, it is also the first to organize Jain doctrine in one volume. It opens with "The Three Jewels of Jainism": correct faith, correct knowledge, and correct conduct.

The Digambara Canon

The oldest text in the Digambara canon is the *Scripture of Six Parts*, by Dharasena, an ascetic of the second century; soon after this came Gunabhadra's *Treatise on the Passions*. These are the only two ancient texts accepted by the Digambara, both concerning the nature of the soul and liberation from *samsara*, or suffering.

Later texts over the centuries have been collected in Expositions, consisting of: *Universal History*, the origins and lives of Mahavira and the other *Jinas*, written in the first century by Jinasena and his pupil Gunabhada (the Shvetambara have their own version of this); texts on cosmology; texts on behavior, including texts by Kundakunda, possibly in the eighth century (though the Shvetambara say seventh); metaphysical works; and devotional hymns.

Originally, access to the scriptures was restricted to ascetics and, being written in nonvernacular language, was not readable by laypeople anyway. Indeed, study without the guidance of a qualified ascetic is seen as dangerous. Recently there has been a relaxation of this idea with the publication of edited versions of the scriptures, affording access to more people; even so, much scripture remains exclusive to ascetics.

THE ESSENCE OF JAINISM

The soul of every living thing is trapped in a cycle (*samsara*) of birth, death, and rebirth and suffers because it is unaware of its true nature—omniscience (pure and simultaneous knowledge of everything) and bliss. Only awareness of the soul's true nature provides *moksha*, release from samsara, and the liberated soul (*arhat* or *kevalin*) undergoes no more incarnations and no further worldly entrapment. Moksha leads to a state called *siddha* (the liberated soul), which has no physical body and dwells at the very top of the universe in a state of omniscience and bliss.

Karmic Bondage

What binds souls in samsara is karma: physical matter, a fine, undetectable "dust" that permeates the entire universe. It attaches itself to the soul and obscures the soul's knowledge of its true nature. While the soul is active, performing physical, mental, and verbal activities, it generates energy and this is what attracts the free-floating particles of karma. *Kashaya* (a sort of passion) produces this effect in two ways: attraction to a thing or event and by attachment to it, and aversion to a thing or event. Since all karma binds the soul in samsara, it induces the soul to action, generates energy, and attracts more karma in an increasing cycle of entrapment. Thus all karma masks pure nature in a perpetual cycle of action and reaction. Further incarnations both remove and add karma, and the level of karma accrued defines the nature of the next incarnation of the soul.

One's aim, then, is to escape karmic bondage, to attain moksha and become a siddha, comprehending the innate potential of the soul (*jiva*); attaining enlightenment and omniscience (*kevalin*); and moksha, final release from rebirth. Thus can all beings attain divinity. To this end, Jains adopt a moral framework for life: *Moksha marg*, a fourteen-stage path to liberation.

Moksha marg involves fourteen stages (*gunasthanas*) of purity for the soul to undergo:

1. *Mithyatva*: The soul is in a sort of deluded sleep; wrong belief due to karmic matter.
2. *Sasasvadana*: Beginning to distinguish between truth and falsehood, but often forgetting.
3. *Misra*: An uncertain state, one moment knowing the truth, the next doubting it.
4. *Avirata samyaktva*: The soul has reached the threshold of liberation. In this stage, there is complete knowledge of truth but not strict adherence to the vows.
5. *Desa-virata*: Partial renunciation of the world and strict adherence to the twelve lay vows. This stage is the highest a layman can attain; thereafter all are for ascetics only.
6. *Pramatta-virata*: Restricting last vestments of pride, enjoyment of the senses, of sleep and gossip.
7. *Apramatta-virata*: The soul is absorbed in spiritual contemplation; one is freed from negligence; anger is conquered; faint residues of pride, greed, and deceit remain.
8. *Apurva-karana*: Contemplation of the pure soul begins; pride disappears and the powers of meditation strengthen. This is a particularly elevating step.
9. *Anivritti-karana*: Pure contemplation; freedom from deceit, pride and anger; just a small craving of greed exists.
10. *Sukshama-samparyaya*: All passions are now destroyed or suppressed; gone are the sense of humor, perception of pain and pleasure, fear, grief, disgust; only a faint degree of greed remains.
11. *Upasanta-moha*: A critical point at which greed must be dealt with.
12. *Ksina-moha*: Greed is gone; the ascetic frees himself from *ghatin* karma, the last obscuring karma, and the most difficult to destroy.
13. *Sayoga-kevali*: The soul is omniscient but still in its body, a state known as *arhat*.
14. *Ayoga-kevalin*: The soul is freed from life and involvement in the material world, and there is complete liberation from karma. All karma gone, the soul proceeds to moksha as a siddha. The soul is full of attributes of omniscience and is in a state of complete bliss.

Another difference between the Digambara and Shvetambara sects is that while the former believe women can attain moksha, the latter denies this, which means that a woman must await a further incarnation in male form before liberation. However, in the current cosmic era it is not possible to pass beyond the sixth or seventh gunasthana.

The Soul

All living things have a soul, which activates the body it inhabits. It is the only conscious thing in the universe, and also has energy and can experience bliss, but only liberated souls experience this fully. The universe is full of an infinite number of monads, units of existence, that are eternal. When a living being dies, the soul is immediately reincarnated to occupy another body—which can be of any type, so one must respect all souls, for each has the potential to become a siddha.

All beings can suffer, and to harm another life-form brings an influx of karma. This is why the Jains espouse nonviolence to all creatures (*ahimsa*), which is their chief ethical doctrine. They have consequently earned a reputation for compassion and tolerance.

Jains also believe in *Parasparopagrahojivanam*, the interdependence of all life, since particles combine to make forms, and when they are destroyed they recombine into other forms. They can be neither destroyed nor created: everything is created, everything is destroyed, everything lasts. Creation, destruction, and permanency are simultaneous: when something is created, the old form is destroyed but the substance is inherently present.

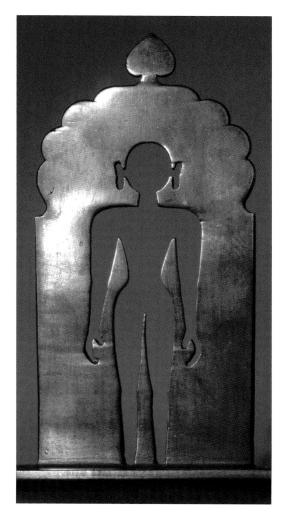

Right: *An eighteenth-century brass icon of great simplicity from Rajasthan, representing the released spirit*

JAIN WORSHIP

There are no priests to act as intermediaries between man and gods, so a Jain is free to worship in a temple or at home. Ascetics have little to do with the temples, which are very much in the hands of the lay community. Jains worship the twenty-four *Jinas* as exemplars rather than as gods, and do not ask for worldly intervention or favors (Jinas are saints who have successfully completed the fourteen steps and acheived siddha). To worship the Jinas, Jains chant mantras and undertake scriptural study. Images can be used in worship according to all except the Shvetambara Terapanthi and Sthanahvasi and the Digambara Taranapanthi. These are in metal or marble, usually in positions of meditation, and appear identical but for their particular symbol (see *tirthankara* chart, page 27). In Shvetambara, Jinas are depicted as nobles, with jewels and crowns; in Digambara, they are shown as naked ascetics. All images are without facial expressions to reflect the fact that they have transcended all human emotions. Devotion is the essence of worship, and offerings are not gifts but renunciations. Rites of puja include:

~ *Darshan*: Gazing at the image in humility and with devotion.
~ *Aarti*: Lighting five little candles, which represent categories of knowledge, on a tray that is waved clockwise while the bearer sings hymns.
~ **The Eightfold Worship** is one of the basic forms. The worshipper bathes and changes his clothes; bows before the image; bathes the image; waves a lamp before it; and then performs spiritual veneration and sings hymns, including the *Panc* (or *Pancha*) *Namaskara Mantra*.

JAIN FESTIVALS

Jain festivals generally commemorate the *tirthankaras*, with ceremonies at their temples. Fasting is also a general practice.

~ *Paryushana* (*Pajjusana*): This is the most important of Jain festivals and ends the Jain year. Held in August and September, it is a time of atonement, to shed the karma of the previous year, and lasts eight days (Shvetambara) or ten days (Digambara). The final day (*Samvatsari*) is the most important, a time of forgiveness (by letter or visit) so that no grudge or quarrel is carried into the new year. Shvetambara consider Samvatsari as their final day, while Digambara consider the twelfth day, *Chemavani*, as the most important day for their sect.

~ *Divali*: This is the Hindu festival of Lakshmi, the goddess of wealth; the Jains also subscribe to this, combining it with the celebration of Mahavira's passing to moksha. On the first day, Jain women polish their jewelry; on the second they propitiate evil spirits with sweetmeats; and on the third day account books are blessed, the Jain finally closing his book and uttering the words "a hundred thousand profits."

~ *Akshayatritiya* (The Immortal Third): This is held on the third day of the waxing moon in the Jain month of Vaishakh (April/May) and commemorates the first giving of alms to Rsabha, the first tirthankara.

~ *Mahavira Jayanti* is Mahavira's birthday, in March or April.

Jains also place great emphasis on the value of pilgrimage, which is usually to the site of a tirthankara's birth. To organize a pilgrimage is seen to be of very great merit to the layman. Pilgrimage destinations include Sammeta Shikhara and Pavapuri in Bihar, Shatrunjaya in Gujarat, and Mount Abu in Rajasthan.

Above: *Shantinatha, sixteenth Tirthankara of the present age*

Above: *One of the temple's many domes in detail*

THE ESSENCE OF SIKHISM

There is a relative simplicity to Sikh belief, because they eschew the idea of prophets, multiple gods, and idols.

God and the Universe

Sikhism is monotheistic, believing in *Akal Purakh*, the oneness of God who is the single divine source of all. God's name is his word (*nam*) and he is without form (*nirankar*), being neither male nor female, not born and never dying. Images and idols of God are frowned upon. God is the eternal truth (*ad sach*) and, while all else in the universe inevitably perishes, God alone continues to exist. God is omnipotent, omniscient, and omnipresent. He is the supreme spirit, the ultimate spiritual reality; he dwells in every soul.

Alahi Hukam

Having created the universe, God set it in order and keeps it so. *Hukam* is the divine order to which humankind must adhere, submitting to the will of God without questions or doubts. Sikhs stress the need to see the divine in the created world. The universe is endless, limitless, boundless and altogether beyond human comprehension. Humans alone of the creatures of the earth are able to see the difference between good and evil, and they can determine their own destiny within the divine order: evil deeds will beget bad consequences for the perpetrator; justice and truth will ultimately prevail. One's destiny is determined by karma, which can be changed, but the key is to live in harmony with hukam.

Haumai

Haumai, "I-me," is self-centeredness, a source of evil and its karmic consequences, and separates humankind from God. It can be classified as greed, lust, pride, anger, or attachment to earthly values.

Humans are thus condemned by egotism and self-will, compounded by a lack of awareness of the divine order. Mastering haumai requires a conscious effort and the adoption of five positive attitudes (with no consideration of consequent reward):

~ Compassion
~ Humility
~ Contemplation
~ Contentment
~ Service, or *seva*, which is seen as the truest form of worship

Mukti

Mutki ("liberation," "salvation" in Punjabi; *moksha* in Sanskrit) is salvation, and for Sikhs, salvation is by enlightenment rather than by redemption. One must listen to the True Guru, who lies within the heart, and meditate with love on the Divine Name. Enlightenment can only come through the grace of God. Through enlightenment, one attains freedom from the cycle of birth and rebirth, and joins the saints in eternal singing of praises at the court of the Immortal Being—one merges with God.

But a righteous life is no guaranteed way to salvation; the coming of the inner True Guru to the individual depends on gaining the favor of the Immortal Being. For this, the individual must prepare the way. Elaborate rituals and extreme asceticism are rejected. Instead, living normally is important, fully engaging in this world, living honestly and supporting others, and meditating lovingly on the divine reality. To avoid the endless cycle one must search for the ultimate spiritual reality by:

~ Leading a life according to the teachings of the gurus.
~ Being honest, believing in the oneness of God and the equality of humankind.
~ Adopting a *kirat karna* lifestyle, living honestly.
~ Performing *chhakna*, sharing with others.
~ Meditating upon mastery of the self by spiritual experience, which involves repeating the divine name and chanting passages from the scriptures.
~ Having faith in the *gurbani*, the words of the gurus.
~ Avoiding being self-focused (*manmukh*) and instead always be *gursikh* (guru-focused).
~ Eschewing lust (*kaam*), anger (*krodh*), greed (*lobh*), attachment to worldy things (*moh*), and ego (*ahankar*) to attain liberation and become a *jivan-mukta*. A *jivan-mukta* is likened to a lotus, being clean despite living in muddy water.

A gursikh becomes a *jivan-mukta* by leading life unmoved by worldly temptation, yet remaining engaged in society, especially by undertaking service. Mukti is the final spiritual release whereby the soul merges with the Supreme Soul (*Paramatma*). The soul (*atma*, or *jot*) is immortal, but the body perishes (the Sikhs believe in cremation). The atma either enters another form of life according to the karma of the individual or merges with the immortal soul in the Realm of Truth (*Sach-khand*), where all disharmony ends. Most Sikhs see this as a heavenly abode to which the spirit goes at physical death rather than the mystical transcendence of death.

Society and Duties

Sikhs must participate fully in society and not become passive as ascetics or yogis who abdicate responsibility and human social life. Renunciation of the world is much against the Sikh way of life—all but one of the gurus was married, living in the ideal "householder" way (*grihsth-ashrama-dharma*). All are equal in the sight of God, and the Sikh's life must reflect certain principles, which include:

~ *Sangat*: All can meditate together
~ *Pangat*: Equality, promoted by sitting together and eating before and after worship
~ *Langar*: Free distribution of food at temples

In sum, the social duties of a Sikh are:
~ *Nam japna*: Always keeping God in one's mind
~ *Kirtkarna*: Earning a living by honest means
~ *Vand chakna*: Giving to charity
~ *Seva*: Service to all

Relationship with Other Religions

Sikhs do not attempt to convert people to Sikhism, preferring cooperation and inter-faith dialogue; they see each religion as having evolved according to its specific cultural background, but all are in fact the same thing, for all humankind has but one creator and nourisher.

However, early on in Sikh history there was a tendency to revert to Hinduism, and in practice, Sikhism never totally succeeded in freeing itself from Hindu influence. The caste system was never totally eradicated; marriages within Sikhism have been constrained by a new caste system, and Untouchables converting to Sikhism are still seen as undesirable in marital terms. Indeed, taboos against eating with Untouchables persist, and in many villages separate wells were dug for them, while in temples there are separate eating places.

Within a century of the death of the Tenth Guru, ritual in temples began to appear very similar to that in Hindu temples, and during the corruption of temples run by *mahands*, Hindu priests often officiated at weddings and funerals. After cremations, ashes were deposited in the Ganges, and at the cremation of Ranjit Singh (founder of the Sikh state), his widows were burned as well. Nor was the special status of cows left to the Hindus; in 1871 cattle slaughter became such an issue in the Punjab that violence got out of hand, provoking the authorities to the outrageous act of executing without trial more than sixty Sikhs of the Kooka movement.

Left: *Worship in a gurdwara*

Below: *The Sikh flag*

SIKH WORSHIP

Individual worship generally consists of reading from the scriptures and reciting hymns (*path-karna*), the *Guru Granth Sahib* always at the core of these practices. Sikh householders keep *gutka*, collections of hymns wrapped in cloth, and frequently keep a copy of the *Adi Granth* at home, often as a private shrine in a separate room. The *Rahit Maryada*, the Sikh code for individual worship, sets out a routine for daily prayer (*nitnem*), including bathing before worship, singing hymns, and ending with *Ardas* (petition), which also concludes congregational worship. Evening prayers include *Rahiras* and *Sohila* (hymn of joy).

There are special services for the traditional landmarks of life. At birth, the naming ceremony (*nam karan*) involves choosing the baby's name by the first letter of the child's birthday *Vah* (see below); in adolescence there is *Amrit Sanchar*, initiation by the *Khalsa* ceremony, when the new adult promises to live according to the *Rahat Maryada*. Weddings are grand affairs—marriage is traditionally between members of the same caste, but the bride is often from a different village from the groom—and the central ceremony includes readings and hymns and concludes with the couple circumambulating the *Adi Granth* four times. Funerals are by cremation, the ashes consigned to rivers.

Priesthood

In Sikhism, there are no monks or priests. Temples were originally run by local elected committees answerable to the community they served. All adults, irrespective of sex or station, can perform religious ritual.

However, a class of professional scripture readers, called *granthis*, developed, together with musicians (*ragis*) to accompany the hymns; these functioned mostly in the big cities where larger congregations made some sort of formal organization necessary. In time, however, control of the temples became a vital issue in Sikh history, settled only in 1925 with the passage of the Sikh Gurdwaras Act, which invested control of temples to a committee.

Congregational Worship

There is no fixed day for worship, but diaspora Sikhs generally worship on a Sunday. Upon entering a temple, a Sikh makes an offering and bows to the *Guru Granth Sahib*, then sits, never turning his back on the book. A service normally includes hymn singing (*shabad kirtan*), accompanied by the music of the ragis and readings from the *Adi Granth* while a ritual fan (*chaudri*) is waved above it. Read first is the *Hukam-nama* (the divine order for the day) or *Vak*, a randomly selected hymn. At the end of the service, sanctified food (*karah parshad*, a sweet pudding) is distributed to the congregation, and then a *langar* (communal meal), symbolic of the Sikh value of equality—food being "a great leveler," on which Guru Nanak laid great emphasis.

Sikh Temples

Dharmsala was the first temple to be established, founded by Guru Nanak in the time of the first five gurus. The major temples (*gurdwara*) have been built on historic sites, where events of special significance have taken place. The *Guru Granth Sahib* is kept within each temple and brought out for services, to be placed upon a raised and cushioned dais beneath a decorated canopy. Here the scriptures will be read.

Above each temple flies the *nisan sahib*, the Sikh flag, which is triangular and saffron-colored with the *khanda* emblem in the center. It is replaced each year at *Baisakhi*, the Sikh New Year.

The Harimandir Sahib, also known as the Golden Temple, at Amritsar is the most sacred site in Sikhism. It has four doors facing in different directions, symbolizing that all are welcome to enter. There are also five temples that are seats of spiritual authority:

The Five Takhats

These five temples are of special importance, for decisions taken by the *sangat* (congregation) here are considered authoritative.

~ *Akal Takhat* at Amritsar, opposite the Golden Temple, was founded by Guru Hargobind and is the largest and oldest of the five. It has preeminent status in terms of Sikh temporal power.
~ *Takhat Sri Patna Sahib* is at the site of Guru Gobind Singh's birth.
~ *Takhat Sri Keshgarh Sahib* at Anandpur is where the *Khalsa* was inaugurated.
~ *Takhat Sri Hazur Sahib*, Nanded, is where Guru Gobind Singh incarnated the guruship in the *Guru Granth Sahib*.
~ *Takhat Sri Damdama Sahib*, near Bhatinda, is where Guru Gobind compiled the final version of the *Guru Granth Sahib*; the temple was declared *Takhat* by the SGPC in 1966.

THE FOLLOWERS OF CONFUCIUS

Zisi

Zhongyong (*The Doctrine of the Mean*) is traditionally attributed to Zisi, a disciple and grandson of Confucius. Its basic messages are that to ascertain the right course of action to follow the Way of Heaven, one should avoid the paths of excess on the one hand and insufficiency on the other, and instead choose the middle way—in other words, follow the basic norms of human activity, which would bring harmony with the Heavenly Way. To do this required *qeng* (sincerity and integrity). However, in its basic forms the right way could be understood by all; in its higher forms it would be beyond the comprehension even of a sage.

Mozi, or Mo-tzu (Teacher Mo), alternatively Qen Huali

Mozi, one of the "hundred philosophers" during the period after the death of Confucius, lived at about the same time as Tsu Ssu, 470–380 BCE, and his school of thought was greatly influential for some two centuries before splitting into three factions. He began as a Confucian but grew critical of several aspects of Confucian thought:

~ Confucius's disciples had emphasized ritual, but Mozi began to see that many of these practices served no purpose.
~ The stress on filial piety and family relationships he saw as restricting: love must be extended to all.
~ He also perceived a failure to denounce the waging of aggressive war.

Mozi did not care for what seemed to be a fatalistic outlook among the disciples of Confucius—while there is a Heavenly Law, man is master of his own destiny. On the other hand, he disliked its apparent agnosticism. Indeed, he was a great believer in Tian and the Way of Heaven, and his teaching was based firmly on this: man is accountable to Heaven for his actions, and the spirits enforce the heavenly law and its consequences. However, while Heaven loves all men impartially, men do not love one another altruistically, a factor resulting at least in part from an overwhelming concern for one's own family or clan. So his essential teaching was the doctrine of universal love—it is in an individual's own interest to follow the way of love for all mankind, and the worth of an action is what it produces rather than its intrinsic value.

Seen as utilitarian in outlook, Mozi was concerned with humanity's well-being in material terms, and he saw rites and sacrifices as valuable in promoting social cohesion.

However, Mohism was also seen as interpreting the teachings of the ancient sages without regard to the emotional requirements of man's nature, and its impartial, universal love could be construed as destructive of the hierarchy of family and state.

Mengzi (Latinized as Mencius)

Mengzi lived from about 372 to 289 BCE (or possibly twenty years earlier) and studied under Zisi. An interpreter of Confucianism, he also traveled from state to state and, like his master, found that those in power would not listen to him. However, by the time of the Song dynasty (960–1279) he was highly esteemed and seen as second only to Confucius. His eponymous book was studied by all scholars, together with the *Analects*, *Zhongyong*, and *Da Xue*, and many centuries later, in 1315, the Mongol overlords included it in their civil service examination curriculum.

Fundamental to the teaching of Mengzi is the concept of humankind's innate goodness. Heaven has given human beings a propensity for benevolence, proof of which is not difficult to find—for example, in the instinctive sympathy people feel for others who are in trouble. His concept was that the *xin* (heart, mind) has innate knowledge of *jen* and *li*, and there exists a

power within all humankind that he called *hao jan chin ch'i* (floodlike energy), an overflow of moral energy and an intrinsic strength that needs constantly to be nourished.

Tian has imbued humankind with four latent virtues upon which one can build: *li* (propriety); *yi* (duty, proper behavior, or righteousness), as emphasized by Confucius; *ren* (benevolence); and *shin* (practical wisdom). These need to be encouraged to grow toward *zhi* (knowledge of right and wrong). By cultivating these inherent qualities, a person may conform to the will of Heaven. On the other hand, evil is due to a lack of proper spiritual nourishment and care.

It follows, therefore, that all political and social institutions are for the good of the people, and that only a sage king is suitable to rule. Indeed, the rise and fall of dynasties may be interpreted in moral terms. A ruler must follow the *Wangdao*, the Emperor's Way—if he does not, the people should rise up against him, for he has forfeited the Mandate of Heaven.

Xunzi, or Hsun Ch'ing, alternatively Xunzi

The third great Confucianist expanded upon the part of Confucius's teaching that leaned toward the rationalistic and humanistic. Xunzi was of the generation following Mengzi and lived from about 300 to 230 BCE, near the end of the period of "the hundred philosophers." He exerted a greater influence than Mengzi during the Han dynasty (206 BCE–220 CE), and his interpretation of Confucianism became a set book for officials. Indeed, his teaching remained the dominant form of Confucianism until Neo-Confucianism in the eleventh century.

Fundamentally, he rejected superstitions. He saw divination as merely pandering to the beliefs of the people; nor were prayers and sacrifices of value. He did not believe in *shen* (spiritual beings) or life after death, nor in *gui* (ghosts). However, he conceded that there was a natural law regulating the universe; for him, the concept of Heaven represented an unknown element in the natural process.

In contrast to Mengzi, he held that the nature of humankind is not good but evil. *Xing* (human nature) tends toward the attainment of self-advantage and pleasure, so if humans followed their latent nature, there would be anarchy and chaos, requiring a strong, authoritarian government to hold such tendencies in check. A person's good or bad fortune was the result of his or her own actions, but he or she could be educated away from this suicidal selfishness—humans, having an intrinsic capacity for knowledge, could learn by conscious activity (*wei*). Rites and ceremonies could play a part in this, both as poetic expressions of humanity's conformity to the natural law and as instruments in teaching people how to conduct themselves. Besides, there was an emotional aspect to such practices that fulfilled other human needs. Thus, while Mengzi's idealistic teaching favored *jen* and *yi*, Xunzi's materialistic interpretation stressed *li* and the need for education.

While Xunzi's message about the need for strong government found acceptance by the ruling classes, his humanistic, antispiritual viewpoint was not recognized by the common people, who held on to their ancient beliefs.

FENG SHUI

Feng shui (winds and waters) is the ancient art of geomancy, or divination based on patterns using the Five Elements, yin-yang, and the Neo-Confucian cosmography to identify auspicious sites for buildings, temples, and graves. By this means one maximizes the benefits of qi, the vital breath, and the natural forces of the landscape. Yang in the form of the Azure Dragon should be to the right; yin, the White Tiger, to the left. A more consumerist modern version has become fashionable in the West.

DAOISM

Origins

Laozi, or Lao-tzu, or Lao Tan (Old Master), reputed author of the *Dao De Jing*, or *Tao Te Ching* (*The Classic of the Way and Its Virtue*), was said to have lived about the same time as Confucius, during the sixth century BCE, but it is probable that he is a legendary figure. What little is known of him is mythic: his prolonged gestation and birth white-haired; that he was an official of the Zhou court and that he met and instructed Confucius; and that, despairing of the court he set off to the west, where the frontier guard persuaded him to write down his teachings. In fact, the majority of the texts in the *Dao De Jing* consist of ancient oral traditions, and later scholarship has ascribed the *Dao De Jing* to an anonymous writer of the fourth century BCE. Nevertheless, Laozi became the traditional founder of Daoism and was himself deified in the second century CE as Lao-lun, human incarnation of the Supreme One.

The teachings of Laozi are said to date from the fifth century BCE, but their authenticity is doubtful. He taught that everything is in perpetual transformation and that the ultimate basis of all is something that differentiates into:

~ *Qi* (breath, vital force, influence)
~ *Xing* (form)
~ *Ji* (matter)

Zhuangzi (Chuang-tzu), generally considered the greatest of Daoist thinkers, lived during the fourth century BCE (possibly 370–286 BCE). His teachings are preserved in a book compiled later, the first seven chapters of which are thought to contain material written by Zhuangzi himself. Much is similar to the *Dao De Jing*, but the emphasis is more personal and mystical.

Daoism as a religion came about during the first half of the second century, when Zang Dao Ling, a preacher/shaman, had a vision of Laozi, who accorded him the title of *Tianshi* (Heavenly Master), the power to heal and fight evil by using Laozi's teachings, authority over spiritual forces, and the key to immortality. Traditionally this vision dates to 142 CE. In effect, Zang was combining the teachings of Laozi with ancient shamanism and the quest for immortality. While an early emphasis of Daoism was disdain for wealth and power, life was seen as the greatest of all possessions, so one must nourish it. However, life is but an incident in an eternal process of transformation; one must accept change as the natural course of things, which implies acceptance of death. Even so, the more popular quests for longevity and immortality gradually assumed increasing significance.

The Essence of Daoism

The basic concept of Dao predates even Laozi, but there is no conclusive evidence of this. Some elements of it were said to originate with the legendary Yellow Emperor Huangdi (mid-third millennium BCE), while generations of *yin zhe* (hermits and recluses) seeking to nourish their inner life began to conceive of the idea that behind everything is *Tai Yi* (a Great Unity) or Dao, an eternal unchanging principle.

Dao is often described as the one universal principle, the very origin of nature, the foundation of all reality—in fact, the Ultimate Reality. It is the unchanging unity beneath all the cosmos and is the impetus to all forms of life and motion. It is more abstract even than nonexistence. Dao produces and sustains all (but without purposeful action) through *te*, the energetic initiative of creativity. Life sprang from nonbeing and must return to nonbeing. In more overtly religious terms, the soul is an emanation from God, who can be equated with Dao.

Like Confucius, Laozi seems to have been concerned with the good governance of the land, and his teaching was directed at the king rather than the mystic hermit. He taught:

~ Conformity with nature. The actions of nature are manifestations of the Dao, which must be emulated.
~ The relativity of good and evil.
~ The strength of "nonaction," naturalness, spontaneity, and passivity, expressed as *wu wei*—being and action that "goes with the flow" instead of constantly striving against it.

Zhuangzi did not address his work to the "sage king"; on the contrary, he saw the implications of *ziran* (naturalness) and *wu wei* as separate from public administration.

To Reach Dao

The goal of a Daoist is to become one with the Dao, achieved by modeling oneself on the Dao, being natural and spontaneous. It can be attained by all. One must embark upon a mystical quest through asceticism and other means to find serenity and know

---

THE TWO ASPECTS OF DAO

Dao has two meanings:

~ Originally it was seen as a spiritual force that pervades the universe, influencing everything within it.
~ Later its name was used to refer to the spiritual discipline, or "way," whereby one can understand the Dao and be absorbed in it.

DAO DEFINED

The origin of Heaven and Earth is nameless. It is indeed nonexistence, something quite indefinable, which, when we attempt to define it, becomes nothing. If we must name it, we may call it *Dao*. It may seem to be prior to God. It becomes nameable in relation to the universe that springs from it, in an order that may be partly known. Not only is it the origin of the universe as a whole, but it presides over all beginnings, reaching everywhere and doing everything, while it seems to do nothing.

Thus *Dao* is indefinite. *Dao* struggles to express this with negatives. From this indefiniteness emanated the universe of all things. *Dao* is working and producing and perfecting all. It is pure being, endowed with spontaneity, the ultimate essence and impulse of all definite things. It is the universal principle. Know the *Dao* and you know everything.

Right: *The Tin Hau temple on Lamma Island, Hong Kong*

Above: A household shrine, here affixed to the exterior, with roof and pot of incense sticks. Incense (hsiang) is thought to help the adherent to the realization of the Dao. Incense is also used to ward off disease and evil spirits.

THE FIVE ELEMENTS: WU HSING

These form the basis of the universe, and they dominate both natural and human events.

Element	Quarter	Represent
Wood	East	Spring and production
Fire	South	Summer and heat
Earth	Center	The natural benefactor
Metal	West	Fall and destruction
Water	North	Winter and cold

---

the perfection of the Dao; only by reducing passions to a minimum and stilling the soul can one become perfect. The Way is to follow nature's path. Zhuangzi stressed the intense spiritual discipline and profound meditation necessary to "return to the root" of all, and he discussed the concept of "fasting the mind" (*xinzhai*), concentrating to attain inner emptiness, as well as careful, unattached wu wei.

To this end, Daoist practices also include attention to inner hygiene by means of careful diet (abstaining from cereals, for example, since these generate malevolent bodily demons) and exercises. Meditation can include the visualization of the Three Divinities, allowing them to descend into one's body, where they reside in the head, heart, and behind the navel; this strengthens the body and wards off disease. The proper circulation of the breath through the body calms the mind and empowers all the parts of the body, while withholding semen during sex was said to retain energy.

Immortality

The search for longevity and immortality was at odds with the original concepts of Daoism but became increasingly popular, with a greater tendency toward superstition, ritual, and the espousal of alchemy. Immortality was thought to be possible by eating certain refined metals. Foremost among Daoist alchemists was Ge Hong (*c.* 280–340 CE), author of *Baopuzi* (*The Book of the Master Who Embraces Simplicity*). The first emperor (221–209 BCE) was obsessed with attaining immortality, and during the Tang dynasty several emperors died as a result. Gold and cinnabar (a form of mercuric sulphide) were thought to

restore imbalance between yin and yang within one's vital energies. Such "outer" alchemy (*wai-tan*) developed into "inner" alchemy (*nei-tan*), whereby the process became a metaphorical, interior purification process.

Buddhism was a challenge to Daoism, but was also an influence upon it. Indeed, one version of the Laozi story asserts that his travels to the west took him to India. Certainly there are striking similarities in the two religions, such as the use of meditation, the emphasis on breathing exercises, and the freeing of the mind. Daoist scriptures became organized into three parts, like the Buddhist *Tripitaka*; and practices in Daoist monasteries and nunneries were similar to those in Buddhist establishments.

Popular Daoism incorporated the ancient belief systems and gradually coalesced into a definable religion with six generally recognized attributes:

~ Ancient quietism, a passive acceptance of the will of God
~ The practice of meditation, which became increasingly complex
~ Breathing exercises
~ Attention to dietary constraints
~ Alchemy
~ Elements reflecting Buddhist influence

Emperor Gaozong (649–83) decreed that each prefecture in China should have state-sponsored Daoist and Buddhist monasteries, which offered protection to such establishments but also gained a measure of control. Confucianism, Daoism, and Buddhism continued as the strands in the tapestry of Chinese religious life, with mutual respect and toleration, right up to the turmoil of the twentieth century.

YIN AND YANG

Dao is the primal source of all, from which come yin and yang. Opposites in perpetual conflict, neither can fully dominate because each contains the seed of the other. By their constant interaction, these two primal and complementary forces, the cosmic souls of the universe, produce all that is—including day and night, the seasons, and their associated phenomena. The summer and winter solstices are seen as especially significant, for it is at these points in the calendar that yin and yang give way to the other.

Yang is male, active, positive, aggressive, and is also spring and summer, light and Heaven.

Yin is female, negative, receptive, passive, quiescent, and is also fall and winter, darkness and Earth.

Creation is an endless effusion and destruction, with never-ceasing reabsorption of particles of yin and yang. Particles, *shen* and *gui*, are innumerable. The former are part of yang and are beneficent, good spirits or a gods; the latter, belonging to yin, are generally spirits of evil, specters, devils, or demons.

Yin and yang contain the Five Elements: metal, wood, water, fire, and earth, and each element possesses a yin and yang quality; all are pervaded by *li*, the natural law, the active principle.

Mankind is composed of the five elements of the *qi* in which li operates and so is in effect a microcosm of nature—a world in miniature. Every human has within him a spark of the divine: in some yin predominates; in others, yang. And, like nature, man has his seasons, his days and nights, and like the world comes to an end by the exhaustion of his *qi*, or vital breath. Humans must fashion their lives to live in conformity with the Tao, the observed order of the universe. The universe is finely balanced and the role of humanity is to maintain that balance by avoiding the creation of excess yin or yang.

THE CHINESE GODS (*TIAN TSUN*, "HEAVENLY HONORED")

The Chinese pantheon is vast and complex, taking in the deities of ancient China—traditional spirits of ancestors, nature, and the household—and with each subsequent religious tradition adding gods or merging identities with existing ones. Deified members of the royal family were joined by scholars and heroes of Confucian history; a plethora of Daoist deities from the Celestial Honored Ones and the Eight Immortals down; while from the Buddhist tradition came Buddhas, *bodhisattvas*, and *arhats*. Many of the Chinese deities were once human but then promoted to the spirit world after death.

Tian (Heaven), the Jade Emperor. Known variously as Yu-ti and Yu Huang Shang-ti (Supreme August Jade Emperor), or Lao-T'ien-yeh (Ancient Ancestor Heaven), this is the supreme Daoist god, the source of power and order in the cosmos, who decides all that happens in heaven and on earth. Buddhist influence divided Tian into various realms, so that the deity became an impersonal power of nature, which Daoists could relate to the Dao. He is associated with the Way of Heaven and the moral, righteous life, and is grantor of the Mandate of Heaven to the ruler of China. Tian is the supreme god of the imperial family and feudal nobility; the Jade Emperor was the popular equivalent. During the Zhou period he was the focus of a state cult, and during the Sung dynasty he became seen as ruler of a heavenly court, with attendant bureaucracy (organized in ministries), mirroring that on earth.

Tung Yueh Ta Ti (Great Divine Ruler of the Eastern Peak), or T'ai Shan. God of a mountain in Shantung, Tung Yueh Ta Ti rules the Ministry of the Five Sacred Mountains (Wu Yo) and is the immediate controller of humanity, determining an individual's fortune and destiny down to the time of birth and death. He is the Jade Emperor's grandson and principal assistant.

Fuxi, **Shennung** and **Huangdi**, the legendary first three "sage emperors," dating from the twenty-eigthth through twenty-fifth centuries BCE, control the Heavenly Ministry of Healing (*Tian I Yuan*). Fuxi (the Ox-Tamer) is venerated as the ruler who taught the people how to domesticate animals, to fish, and to make music. Shennung, the Divine Farmer, invented the plow and market trading. Huangdi, the "Yellow Emperor," was the inventor of warfare and many other civilizing developments, and to him is ascribed the medical treatise *Huangdi Neijing* (*The Yellow Emperor's Inner Canon*).

THE EIGHT IMMORTALS: BA XIAN (PA-HSIEN)

These Daoist deities were originally humans who lived perfect lives and attained *chen jen*, the highest religious ideal. For this they were rewarded by *Xiwang mu* (the Queen Mother of the West) with peaches that gave them eternal life. They are associated with good fortune, specifically with the Eight Conditions of Life (youth, age, poverty, wealth, high and low rank, and masculine and feminine); amulets and charms with their imagery are carried to bring luck.

Cao Guojiu was a historical character who died in 1097 CE and was brother of a corrupt emperor, whom he tried to reform by reminding him of the inevitable laws of Heaven. He is the god of actors and is symbolized by castanets or rattles.

Han Chung-Li became immortal after leading the life of an ascetic in the mountains. He is old and stout, nearly bald and with a waist-deep beard, but always smiling. His symbol is a fan, with which he can raise the dead.

Han Xiangzi is patron of music, portrayed with flute and flowers. A scholar, he is said to have renounced a career in the civil service in favor of music, for which his father reprimanded him; he thereupon magically materialized flowers with leaves on which poems had been written.

He Xiangu is the immortal maiden, goddess of housewives, symbolized by ladle and lotus. She was a Cantonese girl who ate mother-of-pearl powder and dreamed of becoming immortal. She is said to appear only to men of great virtue.

Lan Zaine is a young itinerant flautist, clad in rags, with only one shoe, and carrying a basket of flowers. He is sometimes shown with female features.

Li Tieguai is a healer and purveyor of drugs, which he carries in a gourd; some of these drugs can even raise the dead. Irascible, with an iron crutch, his symbol is a bat.

Ludongbin was born at the end of the eighth century and is a hero of Chinese literature. Renouncing his wealth, he received a magic sword from the fire dragon. This enabled him to hide from death and conquer demons. He is the patron of barbers.

Zhang Guolao was a bat before he took human form. An aged hermit, he is an historical figure of the Tang era and a personification of the primordial vapor, source of all life. His symbols include a bamboo drum and an ass—he owned a donkey that could run incredible speeds.

Right: Kuan Yin, "He Who Hears the Sound of the World," is usually portrayed with female features and derives from the Mahyana Buddhist Avalokitesvara, manifestation of the bodhisattva Amida. In Japan this god is known as Kannon; in Tibet, Pyan-ras-gzigs; and Chenrezi in the West.

Chenghuang is the god of walls and moats, the city god, who protects it from attack and also ensures that the King of the Dead takes away souls only with the proper authorization. All settlements, large and small, had such a god, often a local notable deified after death. He is assisted by a day-watchman (Ba Lao-y) and a night-watchman (Hei Lao-y).

T'u-ti, portrayed as kindly old men, are the popular guardians and protectors of specific parts of habitations, such as streets and lanes.

Zuowang is the god of the hearth, present in every household. He sees all that passes in the home and records each individual's actions; his wife takes note of their utterances. He reports all this to the Jade Emperor, at which time the occupants of the dwelling put sweetmeats in the mouth of his paper image; the paper is then burned, with firecrackers set alight to speed his passage.

Xiwang, the Queen Mother of the West, was revered by nobles and commoners alike. A popular goddess, divine lover, and teacher of humans in search of immortality, she is thought of as the primal breath of the Ultimate Yin. She is portrayed with tousled hair under a distinctive headdress, with tiger's teeth and a leopard's tail. She is often accompanied by strange and wondrous beasts, such as the phoenix and a three-legged bird, and the hare of the moon (equivalent to the Western "Man in the Moon"). She lives in the Kunlun Mountains, beyond the western borders of China, which linked heaven and earth. She cultivates the peaches of immortality, which ripen but once every three thousand years; these she serves to the immortals at a great celestial feast.

Kuan Yin, Hearer of Cries, is the goddess of compassion and mercy, who has a special place in the affections of the Chinese and who protects women and children. Two traditions explain her origins. In one, she was murdered by her father; on arrival in hell she failed to succumb to the malevolent attentions of the rulers of the underworld and was returned to the land of the living and rewarded by Buddha for her virtue with immortality. The other traces her origins to a male bodhisattva, Avalokitesvara, which was introduced to China in the fifth century but misinterpreted.

Ti-Tsang Wang is the god of mercy, a monk of benevolent aspect whose way through the dark regions of hell is illuminated by a glowing pearl as he seeks out souls to save. He even has the power to terminate the cycle of reincarnation.

Caishen is the god of wealth. Mustachioed and dark of visage, he is majestic and dressed in exquisite silks. He presides over a large bureaucracy manned by minor deities and is a very popular god.

Kuan Ti is god of war, a historical figure of the Han period and a warrior of renown. His role is to protect the realm from enemies, both external and internal. There were 1,600 temples devoted to him. He goes by the name of Fu-mo-ta-ti in folk traditions.

Shi-T'ien yen Wang, or Shih Wang, are the Kings of the Ten Hells, lords of death, the ten rulers of the underworld. Each presides over a separate court according to the earthly offense with which a soul is charged; they have the power to sentence a soul to one of the eight courts of punishment and torture. The first king decides whether newly arrived souls deserve punishment, and if they do, decides to which court they should be committed. The tenth king turns the Wheel of Transmigration, which takes the dead to their new stations as animals, demons, humans on earth or in hell, or gods. Before they are released they imbibe the brew of oblivion, which causes them to lose all memory of their previous lives. The Chinese hell is essentially Buddhist in concept but accepted with modifications by the Daoists.

Lei Gong is god of thunder. He carries a drum and mallet to make thunder, plus a chisel to chastise sinners. He punishes people guilty of undetected crimes and also evil spirits who harm humans by means of their special knowledge of Daoism. He is portrayed in fearsome aspect, with claws, bat wings, and a blue body. His assistants are Yu-tzu, or Yu Shih, god of rain; Yun T'ung, god of clouds; and Tien Mu, god of lightning, who produces bolts with mirrors. Another assistant, Feng Po, was god of wind, but was later transformed into the female Feng P'o P'o, who rides a tiger among the clouds.

O-mi-t'o fo, Amitayus, or Amitabha, Buddha of infinite light, who made a vow to save all living creatures. He rules the Western Paradise (the Pure Land), the Land of the Blessed, and is the personification of compassion and the bestower of longevity. His cult emerged in the middle of the seventh century and spread from China to Japan, where it led to the Pure Land and True Pure Land schools of Buddhism in the twelfth and thirteenth centuries.

OTHER LEGENDARY FIGURES WORSHIPPED BY THE ANCIENT CHINESE

~ *Yu Chao*, who taught men how to build houses

~ *Sui Jen*, who discovered fire

~ *Nu Kua*, empress who established the institution of marriage

THE RELIGIONS OF JAPAN

While Shinto has always provided the bedrock of Japanese religion, the Japanese have been able to assimilate new ideas and beliefs in such a way that these new imports did not displace previous religions but were integrated into a sort of homogeneous tradition—harmony and continuity (with several notable exceptions) are the keynotes. The majority of religious ideas, the most important of which are Mahayana Buddhism, Confucianism, and Daoism, have entered Japan via China and Korea.

SHINTO

Shinto is Japan's native, indigenous religion, which has permeated all levels of Japanese society for more than 1,500 years. The word *Shinto* is based on the Chinese characters *shen* (divine being) and *dao* (way), meaning "teaching of the gods" or "the way of the gods." The Japanese probably used to refer to their beliefs as *kami-no-michi* or *Kannaguru no michi* but gave the belief system the name Shinto in the eighth century after the introduction of Buddhism, as a means of distinguishing it from the new arrival.

It is a religion little developed beyond basic polytheism, and is possibly best defined in terms of what it is not:

~ There is no recognized founder.
~ There is no written dogma, no official scriptures, no fixed doctrine.

~ Shinto gods do not have infinite knowledge and power.
~ Celestial bodies are incidental.
~ There is scarcely anything of a moral code.
~ Little attention is paid to any concept of the afterlife.
~ It is not a religion of philosophy or deep theological development.

Indeed, its origins are obscured by the mists of time. It is a conglomeration of practices that include animism (belief in the divine powers of natural forces and in supernatural forces in natural objects) with a strong bias toward ancestor worship. Human deities were added later and remain of lesser importance, and personifications are vague. The influence of Daoism, Confucianism, and Buddhism have augmented and enriched a tapestry of religious beliefs.

SHINTO LITERATURE

Shinto has no philosophical literature or rationale, no equivalent to the Bible, the Qur'an, or the *Adi Granth*, and the literature that exists is not studied by ordinary people. However, several volumes record the mythology of Japan and set out laws for rites and ceremonies. As with other religions, myths and rituals were originally transmitted orally, chiefly by the Nakatomi and Imbe hereditary priestly "corporations" attached to the courts of the emperors. The legends were assembled in two eighth-century collections, Rokkokushi and Engishiki—the first written records of the

Japanese beliefs and customs (writing was introduced to Japan from China in the fifth century). Official compilations, they focused on the imperial house.

Rokkokushi
Known as the Six National Histories, Rokkokushi includes *Kojiki* (*Records of Ancient Matters*), which was written in 712; its narrative ends in 628. *Nihongi,* or *Nihonshoki* (*Chronicles of Japan*), from 720, is a fuller account, ending in 696 with death of the Empress Jito. *Shoku Nihongi* (*Continuing Chronicles of Japan*) was

completed 797 and covers events to 791; three other books take the story to 853.

Kojiki and *Nihonshoki* remain the most important Shinto books, the basis of the Japanese belief system. They contain myths of the transition from divine to human rule, reigns, shrine building (including Buddhist ones), plus worship practices and dances, and *matsuri* (cyclical special worship). These books established the Shinto universe, the creation mythology (see page 32), as well as many other themes, including explanations of the forces of life and fertility, of pollution and purification, the importance of Amaterasu Omikami (the sun goddess), and of the descent of the imperial line from her.

The Engishiki are fifty books on laws written after the Engi Era (901–22) and completed in 927. The first ten volumes cover *Jingi-ryo*, laws on Shinto and shrine ceremonies, plus the duties of the *Jingikan* (Bureau of Kami Affairs). Book 8 contains most of the official prayers and liturgies (*norito*).

Jinno Shotoki is a treatise on politics and history written in 1339, a guide to practice in use up to the Meiji period.

Dai Nipponshi, a history of Japan written by Tokugawa Mitsukuni (1628–1700), provided much of the authority for the reforms of the Meiji period.

Left: *The torii gates of Japanese shrines are of striking character, following a general style with detail variations. This one is at the Itsukushima shrine on Miyajimi Island, near Hiroshima.*

THE ESSENCE OF SHINTO

The basis of Shinto and Japan's folk religions is the concept of the *kami*, the divine beings venerated by the Japanese. Traditionally there are eight million kami, but only a small number are identified by name, with specific activities and needs. In earliest times, the most venerated was the kami of fertility and productivity, *musubi no kami* (the kami of the mysterious generative spirit). The word *kami* means "above" or "superior," which suggests that celestial objects were the first deities.

Kami are very varied and include:

~ Powers of nature
~ Natural objects
~ Sacred objects
~ Divinities mentioned in *Kojiki* or *Nihongi*
~ Legendary or historical personages
~ Other divine beings

Omnipresent in nature, kami are associated with particular mountains or rocks, and unusual features such as caves, cliffs, springs, waterfalls, and trees. There are folk tales about such holy places, which often involve animal possession—foxes, badgers, dogs, and cats that bewitch people (usually men). Shinto was mainly a worship of nature in the distant past, and human deities came later, and were always of lesser importance.

The relationship between kami and humans is termed *Oya-ko* (parent-child), or as or as ancestor to descendant. One prays to the kami for protection and benevolent treatment, but kami are not always all-powerful or all good—while they are generally benign, they can bring about plagues and disasters if offended. There is no evil deity, but Susa-no-wo (Rain Storm) tends to represent evil in general. The number of deities varies, coming and going and being reestablished with a new name, while there are occasionally new gods as well. The kami can have different identities, and can split into two or three. In general, there are two types:

~ *Amatsu-kami*, celestial spirits, eternal, who stay above
~ *Kunitsu-kami*, terrestrial spirits for the benefit or discipline of people on earth

Amaterasu-Omikami is the chief kami, enshrined at Jingu. There are practically no idols—there was no art in Japan before sculpture and painting were introduced from China.

Mitama is the divine presence, the spirit of the kami, conceived as a spiritual emanation from it, which resides in mountains and so on, or in his temple on earth. A kami can have two mitama, a spiritual double, one good, one sinister. In shrines, mitama reside in the *shintai*, or "god body": a stone, sword, mirror, or other object deposited in the shrine, usually in a box that is never opened.

Above: *The kami of Fujiyama, Sengensama*

SHINTO MYTHOLOGY AND DEITIES

Preeminent among the Japanese gods—but not the Supreme Deity—is Amaterasu-Omikami (Heavenly Highest Shining Deity), the Sun Goddess, who was created by the union of Izanagi and Izanami (via the left eye of Izanagi) and given charge of the Plain of High Heaven. The sea and the land of Yomi are beyond her jurisdiction. It was her grandson, Ninigi-no-mikoto, who was sent to rule the earth, and it is through him that the emperors descend, beginning with Jimmu, the first emperor. The principal shrine to Amaterasu is at Ise, but there are many others throughout Japan. The *shintai*, or physical token of the sun goddess, is a mirror called the *yata-kagami*, "eight-hand mirror," or *hi-gata no kagami*, "sun-form mirror," which is kept in a box in the *honden* (innermost shrine) at Ise.

Susa-no-wo is the weather deity, god of the rainstorm and of the underworld. Violent in character, he quarreled with his sister, the sun goddess; his misdeeds brought about the wrath of the other gods and he was expelled from heaven. Although Susa-no-wo comes closest of the Shinto deities to a god of evil, in mythology he appears in benificent aspect in the story slaying the eight-headed serpent of Koshi (after making him drunk) and rescuing a young maiden who subsequently became his wife.

Oho-na-mochi (Great Name Possessor) is one of Susa-no-wo's 181 children, also called Oho-kuni-nushi, (Great Country Master), who lives in Idzumo and, aided by his mitama, sets the area in order. His temple is next in importance to the shrines of Ise and is supposed to be visited by all the other gods annually during the tenth month. His shintai is a necklace of jewels.

~ The dwarf-god, Sukuna-bikona, associated with him, floats over the sea in a tiny boat, clothed in bird skins. These two are said to have originated the arts of medicine and charms to ward off evil. Eventually Oho-na-mochi and his son Koto-shiro-nushi (Governor) agreed with the demands of the gods to give up control of the Eight-Island Country to Ninigi-no-mikoto, who descended on a mountain in Kiushiu, a western island, attended by the five *be*, hereditary government corporations or gilds—Nakatomi; Imbe; Sarume; the mirror makers' *be*; and Toyotama, the jewel makers' *be*.

Tsukiyomi (Moon Reckoner), the moon god, was born from Izanagi's right eye but is not one of the greater gods of Japan, and is rarely referred to in the *Nihongi*. In one story he is the murderer of the food goddess and becomes alienated from his sister, the sun goddess. His shintai is a mirror.

Most mountains in Japan have a deity, but few are of more than local importance; the deity of Fujiyama, Sengensama, is the best known.

Midzuchi (Water Father), or river gods, have no individual names and are usually thought of as serpents or dragons. There are two rain gods, who also have dragon form. All wells have a deity, and it is a custom to make offerings to the house well on the morning of New Year's Day. Wells from which water for the great ceremonies of Shinto are drawn are also worshipped, and even the element of water itself is deified on account of its use in sacrifice.

Kagutsuchi (Radiant Father), or Ho-musubi (Fire Growth), is one of five fire gods, worshiped at Mount Atago near Kyoto, and other places, including the mountain shrine at Kono-Jinja. Here worshippers can obtain charms against conflagrations.

Futsu nushi is probably another fire god, whose main shrine is at Kadori, eastern Japan. He was sent down from heaven to prepare Japan for the advent of Ninigi-no-mikoto. His shintai is a sword, and he is the teacher-god of swordsmanship and *judoka*. Futsu-nushi has been recognized in modern times as a war god, together with Take-mika-tsuchi (Brave Dread Father), god of thunder, whose shrine is at Kashima. There is also worship of thunder under the name of Naru-kami (Sounding God).

Uke mochi (Food Possessor), or Uka no Mitama (Spirit of Food), is the goddess of food. The *sake* god is sometimes identified with the food goddess but is sometimes a distinct deity.

Inari, the rice god, or goddess of foodstuffs, may be seen as a variant of Uke-no-Mitama despite the sex difference; one of the most popular of kami, every village and many houses have small shrines to him—there are around 40,000 recognized shrines. Fushimi, south of Kyoto, has the largest Inari shrine. He dispenses agricultural prosperity and many other things, such as restoration of stolen property, wealth, and domestic harmony. The torii are painted red, and the shintai varies, but often it is a round stone. The fox is associated with him as his messenger or servant and is depicted at shrines, often in the form of stone fox effigies on pedestals before the shrine. This has led to the erroneous belief among some Japanese that Inari is the fox god. Inari is said to have assisted Kakazi Muneika, the most celebrated swordsmith of the tenth century, to forge one of his mighty blades and to have cut the rock with it in order to try the blade. Thus the Inari shrine is highly venerated by swordsmiths and cutlers.

Tree gods, especially in individual specimens of great age, are universally worshipped. A *kami-gi* (god tree) is frequently planted before shrines as an offering. Older records also mention Kukunochi (Trees Father), a god of trees; and Kaya no hime (Lady of the Reeds), a deity of herbs and grasses. These gods are prayed to before cutting wood or reeds.

Houses are deified sometimes as one or two deities, with special sanctity being afforded the central pillar, or "king post." There is also a god of the privy and of the gate, the latter being of some of importance in a palace.

Human Gods

Hachiman, originally Yawata, (Eight Banners), a kami of fishermen and farmers, is now the god of war and peace and accounts for about a third of all Shinto shrines. He is not mentioned in *Kojiki* or *Nihongi* but appeared as a cult in Usa, Kyushu, by the eighth century. Patronized by the Minamoto family in the twelfth century, he is thought to be a human deified, the legendary Emperor Ojin of the second and third centuries. Hachiman was the first Shinto god to be assimilated into Japanese Buddhism, as the bodhisattva Daibosatsu, incarnation of Amida. His principal shrine is the Umi-Hachiman-Gu, where he was seen as the god of war, and where soldiers leaving for battle visited to obtain relics. Today he is more favored in his role as god of peace.

Yamato-dake was a hero prince who subdued eastern Japan.

Temmangu presides over learning and calligraphy and is the special god of schoolchildren and teachers. A statesman born in 845, he suffered slanderous accusations by a rival, which ended in his death in exile. Calamities ensued, and a cult propitiates his angry ghost to this day.

Kunado no kami (God of the Come-Not Place) was originally the phallus, symbol of procreative power. It came to represent lusty animal vigor, foe of death and disease, and was used to ward off pestilence. He is now seen as a guardian kami. He has no official shrines but is visible in the shape of a natural phallus-shaped boulder or carved wooden pillar worshipped by the roadside, especially at crossroads, as the god of roads, the guide and protector of travelers.

Namazu is a giant catfish of popular Japanese mythology who lives under the earth and is restrained with a large stone by the god Kashima, who prevents him from thrashing about and causing earthquakes.

Left: *Kasuga Taisha, Nara, is the tutelary shrine of the Fujiwara, the most powerful family of the Nara and Heian/Kyoto periods (eighth to eleventh centuries). It is dedicated to the kami of Nara and is famous for its 3,000-plus lanterns in bronze and stone, which are lit spectacularly during the Lantern Festivals in February (Setubun, 3rd) and August.*

Above: *Meiji shrine, Tokyo, is dedicated to the kami of the Emperor Meiji (reigned 1868–1912) and his consort, the Empress Shoken. Completed in 1920, the shrine was destroyed by U.S. bombing during World War II and was rebuilt after 1945.*

Above: Yasaka shrine, Kyoto, is also known as the Gion shrine, and is famous for the Gion Matsuri, one of the largest of Japan's festivals.

Above: Hachiman shrine, Kamakura, was built by the first shogun, Minamoto Yoritomo. It contains the shrines of the Emperor Ojin, Empress Jingu, and Emperor Chuai.

Above: Heian shrine, Kyoto. The buildings are in part a replica of the imperial palace of the Heian period. It is dedicated to the first and last emperors who ruled from Kyoto and dates to 1895.

JAPANESE SHRINES AND TEMPLES

Despite the decline in religious observance in Japan, as in much of the developed world, and even after the vast destruction wreaked by bombing during World War II, there are still tens of thousands of *jinja* (shrines) throughout the Japanese islands, many of breathtaking beauty.

Each shrine is unique—large or small, devoted to a local phenomenon, place, event, or legend. Many are home to local kami, where the head of the village (*ujiko*) maintains the local shrine for the tribal deity (*ujigami*); some are of a particular type, dedicated to a specific god; and there are a number of major shrines of national and political significance, such as those at Ise and Yasukuni.

Gongen (local kami) inhabit certain mountains, usually volcanic cones, and many have shrines on their summits, where the worshipper can go for purification and gain heightened spiritual powers. The first practitioner was En-no-Gyoja, during

the seventh century, who sought to harness the strength of mountains for spiritual ends. The Shugendo, or En-no-Ozuna, movement, which he founded, links Buddhism with Shinto ascetic exercises, aiming at enlightenment. *Yamabushi*, or *shugenja* (mountain ascetics), seek spiritual invigoration, exorcise evil spirits, and transmit the will of the kami to local villagers. They are organized in groups called *ko*.

Mount Fuji is the most sacred mountain and was revered by the Fuso-kyo sect, which worshipped Sengen Daishin (The Great Deity of Mount Fuji). Mount Ontake is the second, revered by Ontake-kyo, a sect worshipping Ontake Okami (The Great Deity of Ontake).

In 1872, during the Restoration period, when Shinto and Buddhism were forcibly separated, *shugendo* organizations were ordered to disband, but the essential ideas were transmitted to other, sometimes new, sects, and the practice continues today.

Jingu-ji were Japanese shrine-temples—Tendai or Shingon Buddhist temples often built within the area of the Shinto shrine for Buddhist priests to enlighten the kami by chanting sutras. The earliest was at Ise. Practically all of them were destroyed or renamed during the Meiji anti-Buddhist period (see pages 69–70).

The earliest Shinto shrines were probably the dwelling of the local shaman, and most shrines have taken on a number of striking characteristics. Shrine buildings are all of wood, built form hinoki, the Japanese cypress, and generally follow a characteristic style; the coming of Buddhism introduced more complex and elaborately decorated temples. Typical parts of Japanese shrines are:

~ The entrance to the shrine, often via a long avenue of ancient *sugi* trees (cryptomerias); these evergreen trees are highly esteemed as *sibboku* (divine trees).

~ The *torii* (sacred gate), instantly recognizable and of a consistent style: two uprights with two horizontal lintels. Such gates are not mentioned in the *Kojiki* or *Nihongi* and may have been imitations of Chinese or Indian models.

~ A pair of stone *komainu*, effigies of fearsome beasts, sit on each side of the entrance to the shrine as protection or guardian of the resident kami. At Inari shrines, these are replaced by effigies of foxes (*kitsune*), messengers of the deity.

~ An enclosed sacred area containing a washing place, with clean water and ladles in a *mitarasi* (stone basin), for the worshipper to rinse his mouth and hands before worship.

~ Sacred buildings include the *honden* (the main, or inner, sanctuary) which houses the shintai symbol or *mitamashiro* (spirit substance) of the kami. This area is not entered, as it is the physical location of the kami.

Left: A feature of most shrines is a separate stand upon which one will see hundreds of small wooden plaques (ema). These are sold at the shrine; worshippers write their wish on them and, hoping that the kami will help them, hang them on the stand.

~ Shrines also include the *haiden*, or worship area, the front of which is often decorated with *shimenawa*, thick straw rope, and folded white paper strips (used to designate a sacred area or object). Worshippers cannot normally proceed beyond this area. The shimenawa is credited with the power to avert evil, especially disease. Originally a boundary rope, it has come to be regarded as symbolic of sanctity and derives from the rope used to prevent Amaterasu from reentering the cave in ancient myth (see page 32).

~ Larger shrines have stages for performances of the *kagura* or *kagamada*, a pantomime dance commemorating some incident of the mythical narrative. Dancers usually wear masks, often of terrifying aspect; some shrines have troupes of girl dancers. They derive from Uzume-no-Mikoto's dance before the cave in which the sun goddess hid, to entice her to come out (see page 32).

~ Shimenawa delineate sacred areas, and *sakaki* trees (evergreens) are planted in prominent locations.

ISE JINGU

Ise Jingu is the most important shrine in Japan. It is principally dedicated to the veneration of Amaterasu, the sun goddess, and consists of two shrines: Uji Yamada and Ise in Mie. The shrines are four miles apart at the foot of densely wooded hills, separated by the Isuzu River. The original inner shrine (Naiku) was dedicated to Amaterasu-Omikami, and is traditionally dated to the fourth century BCE, but more likely is from the third century CE. The later Geku (outer shrine), probably fifth century, is dedicated to Toyouke-omikami, the grain goddess (as well as of food and housing), so that Ise combines both sky and earth divinities. There are also shrines to other kami in the grounds. An imperial princess was chief priestess (*saigu*).

The shrines, which are simple and elegant, show no evidence of the influence of Buddhism. They are rebuilt on adjoining lots every twenty years, when the shintai is transferred in the *sengushiki* ceremony, and the old temples are dismantled. The new buildings are exact replicas. Each new rebuilding is held to reinvigorate the kami and gives new life to the imperial line as well as to the harvest. The last time this happened was in 1994; the next, said to be the sixty-second rebuilding, takes place in 2013.

A belief persists in the beneficial effects of pilgrimage to Ise, and these became popular during the Tokugawa period—there were mass pilgrimages in 1650, 1705, 1771, and 1830. The Japanese believe that everyone should visit the shrines once in their lifetime, and when a new prime minister takes office, he visits Ise.

Left: The Naiku, the inner shrine

~ There is usually a holy pond or stream within the area of the shrine, spanned by a sacred bridge (*mikasi*); a good example is that at Nikko over the Daiyagawa River.

Additionally, many of the more important shrines have smaller buildings attached, such as an oratory where the emperor's envoy performs his rites, and *massha*, shrines for dependent or associated deities.

By the nineteenth century the Imperial Household Agency took over the running of all royal tombs, which are sacred. Shrines of a certain size have staff affiliated to Jinja Honcho, the Association of Shinto Shrines, which was established in 1946 to administer 80,000 shrines.

In addition to these temples and shrines, many Japanese households still have private shrines. Before 1945, Japanese houses traditionally contained two altars: *kami-dana* ("to the kami" or "the shelf of god"), associated with life and productivity; and *butsudan* (to Buddha), more associated with death and ancestors. On both altars, offerings of food and drink would be made at the start of each new day. At certain shrines, *ofuda* (amulets or charms), consisting of a piece of wood or stone, or a small sheet of paper bearing the seal of the shrine, can be purchased. These are taken home and placed where their influence is desired—for example, at the door to ward off pestilence, by the fire to avoid conflagration, or on the ceiling to protect against thunder.

Above: Shrines to Inari, kami of rice, are characterized by statues of foxes, which are seen as the messengers of Inari.

JAPANESE WORSHIP AND FESTIVALS

Shinto worship is not generally congregational, but is a very individual practice. Worshippers venerate the local kami, making offerings to it and asking for blessings, protection, and help—perhaps to ameliorate a problem, to alleviate a health concern, or to obtain aid in an enterprise or activity. The procedure usually follows a consistent pattern:

~ *Misogi* (purification) is the vital first step, for evil is seen essentially as pollution or filth, a negative entity that can be removed by *misogi harai* (ritual purification). Good is identified with purity, reverence for which pervades all aspects of Japanese life to the present day. At shrines there are always facilities for this, often in the form of a trough or basin of water and ladles. The worshipper washes his or her hands and rinses out the mouth. In some ceremonies, the ritual purification (*harai*) may be undertaken by a priest, who chants and waves a branch of the sacred *sakaki* (prospering tree), and evergreen pine bush.
~ The worshipper makes obeisance toward the shintai and the door of the inner sanctuary may be opened.
~ The worshipper makes offerings of food or drink in the form of money in a collection box.
~ Hands are clapped or a bell (*suzu*) rung, alerting the kami to the worshipper's presence and invoking its presence; the clapping also focuses the mind and soul of the worshipper.
~ The worshipper bows and communicates his request to the kami, including a *norito* (words to pray for), which consists of

an appeal to the deity; these prayers trace their origins back to those used to entice Amatarasu from her cave (see page 32).
~ He or she claps hands again to end the proceedings, bows in prayer, and leaves.

In addition, there may be more recitation of prayers, as well as music and dancing.

Matsuri

Matsuri, ceremonies and festivals, help to bolster social cohesion and community pride. "Shadow" matsuri are ordinary festivals centering on the shrine rather than the kami, when the principal element is the procession of a *mikoshi* (portable shrine) through the village. In larger festivals (*taisai*), which take place every three years or sometimes more frequently, the mikoshi contains the sacred image of the kami. Matsuri also mark seasonal changes and other events.

~ *Shogatsu matsuri* is the New Year festival, running over the first three days of the year. People clean their houses and put up straw rope, symbolizing the bonds of the household to the kami. They visit their shrine or temple to make offerings and to pray for prosperity and good health in the year to come. There are family meals (*osechi*), traditionally featuring *ozoni* (soup) and *mochi* (rice cakes), and gifts are exchanged. In some cults, the tablets bearing ancestors' names at the household shrine are ritually burned and replaced by new ones. Some people ascend mountains to catch the first rays of the morning sun; and at the shrine feathered arrows may be sold to drive away evil. Paper strips bearing the name of the shrine (*fuda*) are taken home for the coming year, and the previous year's are brought back to the shrine to be burned. *Daruma* (papier-mâché dolls) are also taken and brought back, which originally represented *Daruma/Bodhidharma*, the Zen Buddhist founder.

~ *Niiname-sai*, the harvest festival on November 23, is traditionally one of the most important, when the male celestial kami descends to unite with the female terrestrial kami. The emperor celebrates this by eating and offering the kami newly harvested rice.

~ The Shigon sect has a special ritual involving fire, which has origins dating back to Indian Vedic times. Worshippers inscribe short prayers or extracts from sutras on small blocks of wood, which are piled and then set alight. *Goma* (sesame-seed oil) is poured on the flames to make them dance, and as they rise the worshippers feel themselves lifted to a higher level of consciousness. Priests pass objects through the ascending smoke to purify and protect them, and at the end of the ceremony each attendee is dabbed on the forehead with sesame-seed oil as a mark of protection.

~ *Setsubon*, celebrated on February 3 or 4, is the day before the start of spring and is meant to drive out evil spirits by a bean-throwing rite.

Right: *Yasukuni shrine, Tokyo, commemorates Japan's 2.5 million war dead and was established in 1869 (Yasukuni means "peaceful country"). Since the Meiji period, all soldiers killed in wars are enshrined at Yasukumi and referred to as kami. The shrine has become controversial because among those enshrined here are a number of war criminals; visits of Japanese prime ministers to the shrine have caused international outrage, particularly in China, which suffered at the hands of the Japanese military during the twentieth century.*

JAPANESE NEW RELIGIONS

Since 1800, many new strands have been added to the already rich tapestry of Japanese religious life. These new sects are generally referred to as New Religions. They tend to exist outside temple Buddhism and Shrine Shinto and include a plentiful variety of beliefs. While they share traditional values and elements such as ancestor worship, healing, and shamanism, they can also be seen to represent both continuity and adaptation to the modern world.

There is a great diversity of doctrines. They begin from a common viewpoint, however, and tend to stress core, traditional Japanese values, including sincerity, the pursuit of harmony, loyalty, filial piety, modesty, and diligence. One particular theme is a belief in religious healing and the conviction that illness comes from disharmony. Many of these organizations

have teaching establishments—Sokka Gakkai, the largest, even has its own university and newspaper.

During the first sixty years of the nineteenth century, a number of significant New Religions, all relatively middle-class in origin, were founded, including:

Kurozumikyo was founded in 1814 by Kurozumi Munetada (1780–1850), with an emphasis on healing. It gained government authorization as an independent Shinto sect in 1876 and has since grown to number about 250,000 adherents.

Tenrikyo (Religion of Heavenly Truth) was officially recognized in 1908 and was founded by Nakayama Kiki (1798–1887) in 1838. Its adherents believe in a universe created by Tenri-O-no-Mikoto.

Konkokyo (Golden Light) was founded by Kawate Bunjiro (1814–83) in 1858 and is less Shinto than most such movements, believing in the role of its leader as intermediary between humankind and God (Tenche Kane-no-Kami).

In the first half of the twentieth century, several major New Religions came into being, including:

Reiyukai Kodan (Friends of the Spirit Association) founded by Kubo Kakutaro (1890–1944) and Kotani Kimi (1900–71) in 1925 as an offshoot of Nichiren Buddhism, with veneration of ancestors and the Lutus Sutra as important elements. It was especially successful after the religious freedom following World War II, but subsects broke away from Reiyukai, most significantly Rissho Koseikai, founded by Myoko Naganuma (1889–1957) and Nikko Niwano (1906–) in 1938—*rissho* means "establish authentic Buddhism to secure peace in our land." World peace is one of its main objectives. As in a number of New Religions, it began with certain shamanistic, magical elements but dropped these as it matured and is now a respectable teaching organization. Its adherents now number over 5 million.

Soka Gakkai (Association for Creating Values) is a Nichiren-based movement that grew to include millions of adherents. Originally a lay organization under Nichiren Shoshu (a monastic organization claiming to be sole heir to the teachings of Nichiren), it took its present name in the 1930s, led by Makiguchi Tsunesaburo (1871–1944) and Toda Josei (1900–58). Both were imprisoned by the authorities during World War II—Tsunesaburo died in prison—but the movement expanded rapidly after the war. Aggressively proselytizing, it entered politics with its Komeito (Clean Government) party in 1964, favoring freedom of religion and separation of state and religion—contradistinctive to Nichiren Shoshu, which led to schism in 1991.

Early in the twentieth century, the government began to tighten its control on all religions that were seen as contrary to State Shinto. In the 1930s, with increasing aggression and expansion in China, State Shinto was declared the only religion and the emperor was stated to be both sovereign and divine. The whole of Japan was forcibly converted to this belief system; other religions were persecuted or subordinated. In 1941, the Public Security Law gave authorities the right to destroy any group whose preaching was deemed at odds with emperor worship, and during this period those imprisoned included a number of Christians.

After the country's military defeat of 1945, many restrictions were lifted and in a new atmosphere of religious liberty, hundreds of New Religions sprang up, and temple Buddhism and Shrine Shinto sects closely associated with the prewar regime suffered. The Japanese are still coming to terms with the fact that religion, policed for over a thousand years by the government, is now free. Movements founded or revived during this period include:

Perfect Life Kyodan, a revival of Hito-no-michi Kyodan (The Way of Man Society), founded by Miki Tokuharu (1871–1938). Its central precept involves "living life as art."

Sekai Kyuseikyo (The Religion for World Salvation) was established by Okada

Above: *Fushimi shrine, Kyoto, is famous for its many torii gates.*

Mokichi (1882–1955) in 1926. In a divine revelatory experience, he discovered that he was the messiah for the modern age and established Dainihon Kannonkai, centered upon the bodhisattva Kannon. The Japanese government intervened and he was forced to rename his movement Nihon Joka Ryoho, whose main aim was faith healing, but this later split, creating Sekai Kyuseikyo. Heaven on earth (*chijo tengoku*) can be created with its center at Atami.

Tensho Kotai Jingukyo is known as "the dancing religion" because of its Dance of No Ego, performed to induce trances. It was founded 1945 by Kitamura Sayo (1900–67), whom her followers believe to be the successor to Buddha and Jesus Christ.

Aum Shinrikyo was a more controversial new movement. Ashara Shoko (1955–) founded his first sect in 1986 as Aum Shinsen no Kai, but he underwent a supernatural experience in 1987 and the sect was renamed. It received legal status two years later. The avowed aim of the movement was to seek the truth about the creation and destruction of the universe, but it was controversial from the outset. In 1989 it sponsored its own Shinrito (Supreme Truth) party, but this failed at the ballot box; it then became Armageddonist and started building nuclear shelters. A number of mysterious disappearances and allegations of murders soon brought the sect police attention, but it was in the mid-1990s that it entered the world stage. In 1994, by which time there were reported to

be around 9,000 adherents in Japan and as many as 40,000 worldwide, there was a sarin gas attack in Matsumoto, which killed seven people and injured hundreds. A year later a sarin gas attack was made on the Tokyo subway—this time twelve people died and thousands were affected. Other acts of violence ensued, and Asahara and certain followers were put on trial. Thus far, Asahara and eleven other members have been sentenced to death. In 2000 the name of the organization was changed to Aleph, but this has since split.

Those drawn toward the New Religions include a disproportionate number of women, perhaps compensation for the fact that conventional opportunities for the female sex in Japan remain relatively limited. Personal problems, such as marital issues and health, are often a motivation for joining. Dual and multiple affiliation is not uncommon. But, as in much of the developed world, there is considerable apathy toward religion in Japan. The significance of the religious aspects of weddings, for example, is often ignored or misunderstood, especially by the young. Nevertheless, the old religious traditions persist; millions are affiliated to one religion or another and most Japanese are involved in some sort of religious practice at certain times of the year or of life.

ALTERNATIVE AND NEW RELIGIONS

This look at alternative belief systems and religions cannot hope to cover the enormous number of different beliefs that have sprung up in the last two centuries. It does, however, examine different types of belief systems, such as ufology, as well as some contemporary religions that have their roots in mainstream religion, but have developed quite independent identities.

A COURSE IN MIRACLES

This is a 1,200-page channeled book, divided into three parts: the main text, a workbook for students that contains an exercise for each day of the year, and a manual for teachers.

From 1965 to 1972, Dr. Helen Schucman, a research psychologist who previously did not believe in paranormal phenomena, received this text from an inner voice, and dutifully transcribed it into shorthand. It was published in 1976, and since then has sold over one million English copies and been translated into many other languages.

It is, according to the official Web site, "a complete self-study spiritual thought system." Although it uses the language of Christianity, it expresses a "nonsectarian, nondenominational spirituality" and is therefore a universal spiritual teaching, not a religion. It focuses on the forgiveness of others, which removes guilt and allows one to remember God, and the healing of relationships and making them holy.

AETHERIUS SOCIETY

The Aetherius Society is a worldwide spiritual organization comprised of people dedicated to help heal and uplift humanity through spiritual action.

Like many environmentalists and conservationists, the Aetherius Society sees a world desperately out of balance, ecologically despoiled where millions starve while others squander the earth's resources in unfettered consumerism. Its followers also believe that there is intelligent life throughout the universe; some of the aliens on these planets seek to invade and harm our planet, while our spiritual elders—the Cosmic and Ascended Masters—seek to help humanity heal the earth.

The society was founded in 1955 by the late Western Master of Yoga Dr. George King, after he heard a voice tell him, "Prepare yourself! You are to become the voice of Interplanetary Parliament." King became the mental channel through which the Cosmic Masters could impart their message and their powerful wisdom. These masters include great teachers such as Shri Krishna, Jesus, and Buddha, whom the society believes were Cosmic Masters sent to earth to help mankind.

The society sees "true dedicated, tireless spiritual action for the many" as the solution to earth's problems and has specific tasks to which it addresses itself. Two such tasks include Operation Blue Water, which lessens the harm done to the earth's magnetic field by atomic explosions and humanity's negative thoughts and actions, and Operation Prayer Power, which accumulates spiritual energy so that it may be released to alleviate suffering.

Dr. George King, founder of the Aetherius Society

BREATHARIANS
Now known as the
SELF-EMPOWERMENT ACADEMY

This small, Australian-originated sect was established by Jasmuheen, who was born Ellen Greve, in 1994. After a sacred Prana Initiation by Ascended Masters (including Jesus, Buddha, and Krishna), which included contacting the Divine One Within (DOW) in 1993, she claimed that it was possible to exist only on "pranic nourishment"—light—and that she herself did so. After several of her followers died following her way, Jasmuheen warned that it was essential to be fully prepared but insisted this was the way to abolish world hunger.

In 1999 the Australian documentary TV show *60 Minutes* challenged Jasmuheen to live on prana alone for seven days, on camera. After four days the trial had to be stopped because Jasmuheen was severely dehydrated, on the verge of kidney failure, and was suffering from excessive weight loss.

The Ascended Masters have also given Jasmuheen an eight-point plan to "positive personal and planetary progress," which consists of daily meditation, prayer and exercise, mind mastery, a vegetarian diet, selfless service to others, communing with nature, and singing devotional songs and mantras focusing on the DOW. This leads to personal paradise and, finally, planetary paradise.

Jasmuheen, who failed to live on prana when challenged by the Australian TV show 60 Minutes

CANDOMBLÉ

When African slaves—mainly Yoruba, Ewe, Fon, and Bantu—were transported to Bahia in northeastern Brazil, they brought with them their own pantheon of deities (*Orixás*). Candomblé gradually incorporated many Catholic elements and the Orixás developed dual identities—on the one hand African god, on the other Catholic saint. This syncretism may originally have developed to avoid the intense

Right: Mae Menininha, a devotee of Candomblé, in typical dress

Far right: A sphere depicting the Divine Eye inside the Tây Ninh Holy See

persecution of Candomblé devotees by Catholic authorities and slave owners, but this melding of beliefs was also natural for people who followed polytheist religions. Today there are about 2 million declared followers of Candomblé, but many people who would classify themselves as Catholics will attend Candomblé ceremonies and festivals, and the reverse is also true.

The Candomblé ritual (*toque*) has two parts, one public and one private. First, a private preparation by the priest and initiates includes decorating the house in the colors of the honored Orixá—Oxum, for instance, is yellow or gold; Okossi is forest green—and slaughtering domestic animals for sacrifice and the following banquet. Next, during a public ceremony, the Orixá's priests incorporate their deity and fall into a trance. Once in this state, the priests dance to powerful rhythmic percussion music—a celebration of the life force—songs extol the Orixá's deeds, and the ceremony culminates in a fabulous feast.

There are also particular obligations toward each Orixá, including initiation ceremonies, readings of seashells, and divinations, as well as many private rites.

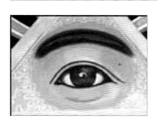

CAO DAI

Cao Dai is a Vietnamese universal faith that believes that all religions in the world have the same divine origin, being different manifestations of one truth. Syncretistic, Cao Dai unifies Buddhism, Taoism, Christianity, and Confucianism into a whole whose principle belief is that "humans shall observe love and justice in order to be unified with God." Its long-term goal is that, through esoteric spiritual self-cultivation, all humanity will escape the tragedy of reincarnation.

In 1920, Ngo Van Chieu, an official of the French Colonial administration, who maintained contact with the spirit world through a mediumistic form of worship, received an apparition from Cao Dai, the Supreme Being. Cao Dai informed Chieu that all the world's religions should return to the One from which they sprang, and the tangible form through which Cao Dai was to be worshipped was the All-Seeing Eye. In 1926, Cao Dai became an official religion recognized by the French administration.

Elaborate festivals and rituals performed in colorful temples are the main form of worship. Séances take place separately. They are the means by which the Supreme Being transmits further sacred messages that become part of ever-increasing teachings.

By 1930, 200,000 Vietnamese were Caodaists, and despite ongoing repression by the French government, the Vietminh (a Vietnamese communist group), and the Catholic Ngo Dinh Diem government, it grew significantly in numbers and influence. In 1975, the Vietnamese communist government severely repressed it and its Cambodian followers were destroyed by the Khmer Rouge. Far from eliminating Cao Dai, these actions spread its message worldwide as Vietnamese and Cambodian diaspora settled in the United States, Canada, and Australia. The religion now claims around 6 million members.

CARGO CULTS

Pacific cargo cults blossomed as a direct response to the presence of outsiders—the introduction of Western-style goods and Christian missionary activity. In general terms, cargo cultists hope for the supranormal arrival of nontraditional Western goods—which range from bully beef to automobiles—that are usually expected to arrive with the collective return of dead ancestors, sometimes with the Second Coming of Christ.

These cults were particularly obvious in Melanesia, (Fiji, New Caledonia, Papua New Guinea, Vanuatu, and the Palau, Torres Strait, Maluku and Solomon

Islands), partially because Melanesian indigenous religions were oriented to the prediction of riches and partially because until the arrival of German steel ships in the 1880s, Melanesia had more or less been free of outside influence. Western-style items came as a sudden, extraordinary revelation.

Cargo cults have many different forms. Some groups, for instance, simply hope for the arrival of ancestor cargo ships across the oceans and watch out for them; others, having noticed that Western-style goods were disgorged from airplanes, built their own runways and control towers and prayed for the arrival of their own metal planes-of-plenty.

Cargo cults are not, however, simply concerned with the arrival of goods. They encompass complex protests and hopes for miraculous transformations, which are occasionally apocalyptic in outlook.

Their dream is that political and religious power be returned to them, that the invaders who have so altered their lives be vanquished, and that their goods be made accessible to all.

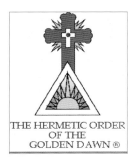

THE HERMETIC ORDER
OF THE
GOLDEN DAWN ®

THE HERMETIC ORDER
OF THE GOLDEN DAWN

Founded in 1888 by the London coroner William Westcott, the Golden Dawn was a classic esoteric order, requiring initiation involving ritual and tests, and claiming a wisdom not available to the mass of humanity.

Temples were established in London, Weston-super-Mare, Bradford, Edinburgh, and Paris with names such as Horus and Osiris. By 1897, there were over 300 members, including the poet William Butler Yeats. Members had to study hard, learn basic ceremonial magic techniques, and obey their leaders. To progress through the stages of the kabbalistic Tree of Life required real dedication, a deep knowledge of esotericism, and proficiency in the theory and practice of magic. Its aim was the philosophical, spiritual, and psychic evolution of humanity.

Strong characters were attracted to the Golden

Dawn—which inevitably led to conflicts and finally to its disintegration in 1903. The original London Temple Isis-Urania became a mystical order, under the esoteric writer Waite. The magical faction of the Golden Dawn reformed as the Stella Matutina and opened temples in New Zealand, London, and Bristol. In 1933 an American, Israel Regardie, joined and, believing that the profound knowledge of Golden Dawn should be available to all, published the bulk of its texts between 1937 and 1940. These have been reprinted often and have led to the establishment of several new Golden Dawn temples. Mainly in America, they continue to disseminate the traditions of Western esotericism and teach the practical applications of ceremonial magic. They emphasize religious tolerance and draw their members from many belief systems and mainstream religions.

KABBALAH

Kabbalah is an ancient, essentially esoteric body of Jewish mysticism. According to many scholars, its first Merkabah expression, in first-century Palestine, was based on the prophet Ezekiel's vision of God's chariot.

Unlike traditional Jewish scripture, which treats the divine as a discrete being, usually named and able to be described in words, traditional kabbalah is concerned with the essence of God—his being, which words can not explain.

Kabbalah, unlike more academic rabbinic Judaism, concerns itself with inner mystical experience and aspiration, which is very often modelled on the ten *sefiroth*, or "tree of life." These ten spheres of energy are symbolic of different areas of God's existence, a map of consciousness and the path to the One.

Contemporary Kabbalah, according to the eighty-year-old Kabbalah Center, whose director is Rav Berg, is not an academic discipline but a means for personal change and transformation. The wisdom of the Kabbalah is to be used to create a better life and to end chaos, pain, and suffering. The center also stresses that every human being has the potential for greatness and that Kabbalah is the means for activating that potential. Many of the rich and famous, including Madonna, find this an attractive concept.

KIMBANGUISM AND NGUNZISM

Kimbangu was born in the Belgian Congo in 1887. Educated as a Baptist, in 1918 God called to him, telling him that European Christians were not faithful to the call of Jesus, and that he should minister to his own people.

On April 6, 1921, Kimbangu's first miraculous healing in the name of Christ took place in his home village of N'Kamba. His healings and biblical teachings inaugurated a mass Congolese movement. Kimbangu's popularity was so great that the Belgian colonialists feared they would lose their authority and a mere five months after his first healing, they flogged Kimbangu, threw him into jail, and declared a state of emergency. Kimbangu was never to leave jail and died there thirty years later. But to his

Madonna is a follower of Kabbalah.

Far left: *Cargo and food being delivered by United States Far East Air Forces Combat Cargo Command transport. Islanders believed that they could summon planes with sympathetic magic.*

Kimbanguan healing

devoted followers he was still a constant companion: not only did he appear in their dreams and visions, but his corporeal self, overcoming mere material constraint, also visited them to offer advice and sustenance.

Kimbangu was a conservative who rejected violence, rebellion, witchcraft, polygamy, magic, alcohol, tobacco, and dancing, and whose services were Baptist in orientation. Nevertheless there are some parallels with the already existing Congolese Ngunzism. Ngunzism consisted of many spiritual leaders who, while adhering to no specific religious framework, all entered trancelike states that involved ecstatic trembling and performed miracles, including healing, in the name of the Christian God. A clue to their character may be taken from the fact that when the Old Testament was translated into Kilongo, a Congolese language, the word "prophet" was translated as *Ngunza*.

As Kimbanguism expanded and legendary tales of Kimbangu grew, so did Ngunzism, with many believing Kimbangu himself would return as the *ntotila*, a legendary figure who would reestablish the Kingdom of Kongo and drive the whites back into the sea. The Ngunzists were more radical and more nationalistic than Kimbanguists; when, for instance, Zaire became independent, they were active in rooting out white missionaries, and they also sometimes charged for healing—something strictly forbidden in Kimbanguism.

Kimbanguists, at this time led by Kimbangu's wife, were harshly suppressed. Between 1921 and 1959, more than 100,000 were deported.

In 1959 Kimbangu's wife died, but under the leadership of her son Diangienda the movement spread exponentially beyond the borders of the Congo. In 1969, it joined the World Council of Churches, calling itself the Church of Jesus Christ on Earth Through His Special Envoy Simon Kimbangu. Kimbangu himself is seen as the Holy Spirit made flesh and his healing powers are thought still to reside in the soil and waters of the village of his birth.

Sunday is set aside for religious worship and prayers. Music, particularly choral music, plays a great part in the services. Many of Kimbangu's early teachings were incorporated into song, and these, too, are often performed during prayers.

Kimbanguism is concerned with the good of the community as a whole, and services end with a collection, the proceeds of which are generally for a specific project, such as a new hospital or school.

Today there are over 10 million Kimbanguists worldwide.

Rastafarian wearing dreadlocks

Ganga (marijuana), favored by the Rastafarians

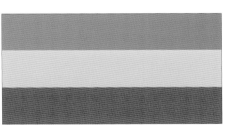

The seal of the Knights Templar

ORDER OF THE SOLAR TEMPLE

This is a generic name for a series of groups formed by the Frenchman Jo Di Mambro. In the 1980s, it was fronted by the charismatic doctor Luc Jouret (1947–94). Springing at first from Western esoteric tradition, highly influenced by Egypt and the Knights Templar, the groups became increasingly apocalyptic in orientation. But Mambro and Jouret initially saw not a divine judgment but ecological disaster, which with the correct preparation could be survived. By the 1990s, the cult believed the only way to survive would be to leave earth.

More advanced members believed Jouret would lead them to a planet orbiting Sirius. Jouret himself, however, gave a hint of things to come when he said, "Liberation is not where human beings think it is. Death can represent an essential stage of life."

Rituals and ceremonies were an important and bonding part of the cult's group life. Prior to their performance, Jouret would have sex with one of the female members to ensure his spiritual strength. During the ceremonies, Di Mambro would be backstage, operating electronic projection devices to give the illusion of supernatural phenomena. In the early 1990s, disillusioned members defected, and Di Mambro's son exposed the trickery to many. This provoked a crisis. Di Mambro and Jouret decided that rather than have their "legend" destroyed, they and their remaining core of members must "transit" to another world. Fifty-three members of the order perished in fires at their headquarters in Switzerland. Initially it seemed that this was a group suicide, but it was discovered that at least twenty-one victims had been given sleeping pills before being shot.

The national colors that appear on the flag of Ethiopia and on that of the Rastafarians

RASTAFARIANS

Forcibly taken from their homeland by white slave traders, Africans worldwide longed for their homeland, and by the 1890s, Back-to-Africa movements were springing up everywhere. This profound longing meant that Africa gradually became seen not just as a country but as a sacred and promised land of peace.

Prominent worldwide in these movements was the Jamaican Marcus Garvey (1887–1940), who told his followers: "Look to Africa for the crowning of a black king; he shall be the redeemer."

In November 1930, Ras (Prince) Tafari (Creator) Makonnen, crowned Negus of Ethiopia, declared he was a descendant of King Solomon and took the names Haile Selassie (Might of Trinity) and Lion of the Tribe of Judah. In this leader many saw the prophesied black king, Christ, returned. Leonard Howel, a mystical Jamiacan, saw evidence for this in Revelations 5:5 and 19:16, and believed Ras Tafari would indeed lead his people back to Ethiopia, symbolic of all Africa.

A small, Jamaican-based religion in the 1930s, by the 1950s enduring poverty and repression had swelled Rastafarian membership in both Jamaica and the United Kingdom. It gave hope and the promise of salvation; the end of the present era of dominating white cultural and religious values and the dawning of a new age of peace and love among men.

Rastafarians, unlike mainstream Christians, do not submit to the authority of the Bible but insist that its teachings be validated by the self, either through "head resting" (meditating) one with Jah, or by group discussions. Rastafarians believe the divine to be within the self, and seek spiritual knowledge, not crystalized belief. Many Biblical passages indicate to Rastafarians that smoking *ganga* (marijuana) is both natural and beneficent, bestowing not only relaxed well-being but inner spiritual inspiration. Ganga is a natural substance, and thus in accordance with the central Rastafarian belief to live in accord with nature and eat only natural, unadulterated foods.

Many Rastafarians are immediately recognizable by their dreadlocks, grown in accordance with the Bible verses of Numbers 6. This profusion of hair resembles a lion's mane and symbolizes spirit, strength, and royalty. It also establishes Rastafarians as standing apart from mainstream mores, and having their own distinctive culture.

Rastafarians number around a million worldwide, the vast majority in the United Kingdom and Jamaica.

SATANISM

Satanism is a term that covers the practices of a number of small groups, the principal of which are Anton LaVey's Church of Satan (established 1966), the Temple of Set and, increasingly, individuals.

Satan is a biblical supernatural entity possessed of demonic powers, but few Satanists would say that they literally worship him. Instead he stands as an icon against establishment Christianity, to be invoked in rituals that decry Christianity, such as Black Masses, as well as a symbol of individuality and the promotion of self-interest.

The latter covers a wide spectrum from LaVey's emphasis on the validity of the natural physical desires of humans, the continuum between man and animals, the emphasis on the survival of the fittest, and the overarching dictum of the charismatic magician Aleister Crowley (1875–1947): " 'Do what thou wilt' shall be the whole of the law." The last is an attitude that appeals to many Satanists.

Crowley used ritual and ceremonial magic to enforce his will, to change the conditions of this material world, and to summon entities from other worlds. Crucial to these rituals was a form of "sexual Magick" that gave added power to his practices.

The temple of Set, founded by Michael Aquino, a onetime member of the Church of Satan, follows these Magickal precepts and sees in Set not a being to worship but one to learn from and emulate.

SCIENTOLOGY

The Church of Scientology (1954) is the invention of its founder, L. Ron Hubbard (1911–86), who stated that its aims were "a civilization without insanity, without criminals and without war, where the able can prosper and honest beings can have rights, and where man is free to rise to greater heights."

Crucial to this achievement is evolution to higher spiritual states—achieved by studying Dianetics. This analysis of the human being concluded that there is a true essential, immortal godlike self, *thetan*. This is neither body nor mind although the body, consisting of matter, energy, space, and time—MEST—is dependent on it. Thetan may be seen as the spirituality of the individual, which modern thought has chosen to ignore, placing all its faith in the material.

Dianetics sees the mind as divided into two parts: the rational analytical and the irrational reactive. The latter is constantly involved with MEST and stores memories, or engrams, of unpleasant events, which cause suffering and irrational fear. A lengthy process known as auditing, conducted by a trained Scientology auditor, identifies these harmful memories and removes them. Individuals are then "clear" and can progress through further spiritual stages, until they become Operating Thetans who are able to control themselves and their environment and know that they are apart from "material things such as physical form or the physical universe."

There are around 5.6 million Scientologists worldwide, and it is worth noting that Hubbard's book, *Dianetics: The Modern Science of Mental Health*, published in 1950, sold over a million copies well before he founded his church.

SPIRITUALISM

Since the dawn of history, humankind has endeavored to communicate with the spirits of the dead and to ask them for advice on earthly matters, using such means as shamanistic trance or ancestor worship. Modern spiritualism, however, has its roots in the work of the scientist and Christian Emanuel Swedenborg (1688–1772), a talented clairvoyant who crucially disseminated the idea that mediumship proved the existence of an afterlife. It only became popular in 1848 after two sisters, Catherine and Margaretta Fox, succeeded in contacting a spirit that was haunting their home. The first publicly recorded instance of spirit communication, it caused a sensation. The pair went on tour to promote spiritualism, and soon thousands of others were trying to contact the dead.

Early spiritualism was physical. Spirits made contact at séances by rapping tables, ectoplasm was often exuded, and usually the spirits communicated

L. Ron Hubbard, who founded the Church of Scientology

Anton LaVey, founder of the Church of Satan

Emanuel Swedenborg

through a trance medium. Later, in the nineteenth century, mediums tended to remain conscious while seeing (clairvoyance) or hearing (clairaudience) spirits and passing on the information they received.

Although there are many Spiritualist churches worldwide, and some make reference to Christianity and Christ's redemptive power, the movement is essentially secular. They are united by the view that the spirit is set free after death and can choose to ascend to a higher spiritual level, reincarnate, or act as a guide to the living. The overall aim is to facilitate communication between their congregation and these guides.

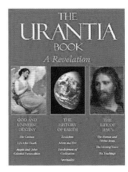

URANTIA

The book *Urantia* was presented by celestial beings to our Earth, known to them as Urantia, in 1934. In it is revealed a complex multidimensional system composed of 10 million inhabited worlds ruled by celestial beings; a detailed history of Urantia since its formation over a billion years ago; and the unique interpretation of the life and teachings of Jesus or Christ Michael, stripped of religious dogma. At the highest level, Paradise is I AM. When we die, our souls undergo a lengthy journey of self-discovery but eventually reach Paradise.

Christ Michael is one of 700,000 Creator Sons incarnated throughout this universe. These sons are material representations of the Universal Father, God. God himself is constantly with each person, through his indwelling spirits, the Thought Adjusters, who seek to guide humanity to spiritual truth.

The Urantia Foundation has no system of churches—its membership's sole activity is to study the book *Urantia*, which itself encourages a "personal, living religious faith."

For Urantia, the great hope is that when Jesus returns to Earth it will be with a saving revelation that will at last spiritually unite all humanity in loving service.

Many Wicca followers honor the triple goddess of the full, waxing, and waning moon.

VAMPIRISM

The vampire is an enduring and haunting image in Western society. For members of the Temple of the Vampire, founded in 1989 by Lucas Martel, vampires were the old gods, such as Osiris and Isis of ancient Egypt. According to this temple, ancient records say that humans were their servants and charged with bringing them an Elixir of Life, which went by various names, including blood and ambrosia. But when these early priesthoods collapsed, "Those Who Came Forth to Feed upon humankind came to be known as Vampires."

The Vampire Bible

Dayside Vampirism—that which deals with the living in the world—concentrates on ruthless materialistic mastery, the creation of wealth, and the ability to control others. Nightside Vampirism insists that everything be questioned and tested by rational scrutiny and the development of true vampire powers, which include shape-shifting, flying, mesmeric power, and communion with the Undead Gods.

The Temple of the Vampire seeks membership only from those "born to the Blood." Such members feel this intuitively and instinctively know they are superior to the bulk of humanity. They are thus drawn to the night and the Temple of the Vampire.

The key elements of this belief system are contained in *The Vampire Bible*, which anyone may read. Further wisdom to progress through the temple's circles is only available to members and is contained in *The Vampire Predator Bible*, *The Vampire Priesthood Bible*, *The Vampire Sorcery Bible*, and *The Vampire Adept Bible*. Worship focuses on the Undead, powerful immortal vampires who are capable of transforming members into beings possessed of eternal life.

WICCA

Wicca has its roots in Celtic, pre-Christian paganism, which celebrates the old gods and nature. The exact nature of Wicca (from Anglo-Saxon *wicce*, meaning "witch" or "wise woman") has been lost due to the Christian church's ruthless suppression of all forms of paganism. It was not until 1951, when the 1735 Act of Parliament banning witchcraft was repealed, that Gerald Gardner (1884–1964), a leading light of one branch of Wicca, was able to publish his seminal book *Witchcraft Today*.

Modern Wicca is practiced in different ways, but all Wicca is nondogmatic, rejects patriarchal monotheistic religions, and generally embraces both gods and goddesses. The members of the American Covenant of the Goddess honor, among others, the Triple Goddess of the full, waxing, and waning moon and the Horned God of the sun and animal life as visualizations of immanent nature. They stress that the way to attune yourself to nature is to experience it. Also integral to Wicca is the belief that everyone can experience the divine mystery, the feeling of ineffable oneness with all life. Some Wiccans believe transformation may be brought about through the practice of "high" magic—rituals and initiations. But Wiccan magic may also, by using natural substances such as herbs and crystals, harness natural or even supernatural forces and use them to make positive earthly changes and effecting healing.

The Covenant of the Goddess Web site, having analyzed a 1999 census, estimates that there are 750,000 wiccans/pagans in the United States today.

INDEX

Aarti, 130
Abba Arika, 40
Abbasid Caliphate, 47, 52, 114, 115
Abd al-Rahman III, Caliph, 47
Abdullah Gu, 80
Abelard, Peter, 49
Abraham, 24, 34, 35, 102, 110
Abu Bakr Muhammad ar-Razi, (Rhazes), 45, 47, 110
Abu Simbel, 33
Abubacer, 50, 51
Abydos, 83
Acarya Bhiksu, 65
Achaemenid Empire, 37
A Course in Miracles, 152
Acre, 49, 53
Act of Supremacy, 60
Act of Uniformity, 104
Adam and Eve, 24, 103, 110
Adena culture, 36
Adi Granth, see Guru Granth Sahib
Adinath temple, 52
Adventist movement, 68
Aelia Capitolina, 40
Aesculapius, 88
Aether, 32
Afghanistan, 78
African belief systems, 92
African Methodist Episcopal Church, 71
Ahimsa, 129, 131
Ahmadinejad, President, 80
Ahmadiyya (Qadi) Sufi sect, 71
Ahriman, 32
Ahura Mazda, 32, 96
Akal Purakh, 57, 132, 133
Akali movement, 70, 71
Akbar, Emperor, 60, 61, 62
Akihito, Emperor, 78
Akkad, 35, 84
Aksobhya, 79
al-Afgani, Jamal al-Din, 71
Alahi Hukam, 133
Alamut, 115
Al-Aqsa mosque, 80
al-Arabi, Muhyi al-Din Ibn, 51, 52, 54
Albigensian crusade, 52
Alcmene, 86
Aleph, 151
Alexander VI, Pope, 59
Alexander the Great, 37, 38, 39, 87, 89
al-Farabi, Abu Nasr Muhammad Ibn Tarkan, 47
Alfasi, Isaac ben Jacob, 48
Alfred the Great, 47
al-Ghazali, Abu Hamid Muhammad, 48, 50, 116
al-Hallaj, Abu al-Mughith al-Husain Mansur, 47
al-Husain, Ali, 44, 45
Ali, 45, 114
Aliyas, 74, 79
Alkalai, Judah, 68
al-Khaliq, 31
Allen, Richard, 68
Almohad dynasty, 50, 51
al-Muqanna, 114
al-Sadat, President Anwar, 79
al-Sanusi, Sidi Muhammad, 68
Altan Khan, 61
al-Tijani, Ahmad, 67
Alvars, 44
al-Wahhab, Muhammad ibn Abd, 67
Amar Das, Guru, 27
Amaravati, 40
Amaterasu, 32, 46, 145, 149
Amenophis IV, Pharaoh, 82
American Muslim Mission, 78
Amiens, 53
Amritsar, 60, 61, 62, 72, 132, 134
Amulius, 88
Amun Ra, 82
Anabaptist movement, 60
Analects, 138, 139
Ananta, 121
Angad, Guru, 27
Angas, 128
Angels, 111

Angkor, 47, 55, 56, 59
Angra Mainu, 96
Angrboda, 91
Annapurna, 122
Anselm, 48, 103
Ansher, 32
Antinous, 89
Antony, 37
Anu, 32, 84, 85
Anubis, 82
Anuvrata, 131
Apollo, 38, 87
Apsu, 32
Aquinas, Thomas, 52, 73, 104
Arafat, Yasser, 79
Arahats, 126
Aranyanas, 36
Ardh Kumbh Mela, 80
Argos, 38
Aristotle, 39
Arius and Arians, 41, 43
Arjan Dev, Guru, 27, 62, 132, 135
ar-Rumi, Jalal ad-Din, 52
Artha, 118
Arti, 123
Arya Samaj, 71
Asgard, 32, 91
Ashkenazim, 47, 51, 68, 101
Ashrama, 118
Ashur, 34, 85
Ashurbanipal, King, 85
Asoka, Emperor, 38, 39, 42
Assassins, 114
Assumption of the Blessed Virgin Mary defined, 76
Assyria, 34, 37, 36
Assyrian religion, 85
Asuras, 32
Aten, 82
Athanasius, 102
Athena, 38
Athos, Mount, 107
Augustine of Canterbury, 44, 45
Augustine of Hippo, 41, 46, 43
Augustus, Emperor, 41, 89
Aum Shinrikyo, 79, 151
Aurangzeb, Emperor, 64, 66, 67
Australia, 93
Avalokiteshvara, 127
Averroes, 50, 51, 54, 116
Avesta, 96
Avicenna, 50
Avignon, 55, 57
Ayodhya, 35, 67, 79, 80
Aztec Empire, 60, 55, 95
Azusa Street Revival, 72

Ba Xian, 142
Bab, 117
Babel, Tower of, 84
Babur, Zahir-ad-din Muhammad, 60
Babylon, 34, 36 , 37, 84
Babylonian Captivity, 55
Babylonian religion, 84
Bach, Johann Sebastian, 64
Baghavad Gita, 39, 78, 120
Bahá'i Faith, 71, 117
Bahá'u'llah, 71, 117
Bai Zu, 136
Bakker, Jim, 79
Balarama, 121
Balder, 91
Balfour Declaration, 72, 74
Banda Aceh, 80
Banda Singh, 64
Baopuzi, 141
Baptism, 104
Baptist churches, 65, 109
Bar Kochba, 40, 41
Bar Mitzvah and Bat Mitzvah, 100
Basil the Great, 46
Basle, 57
Bath, 88
Baybars, 53, 115
Becket, Thomas à, 51
Beilis blood libel case, 72
Beltane, 90
Ben Abraham Adret (the Rashba), 55

Ben Asher, Jacob, 55
Benedict XVI, Pope, 80
Benedict of Nursia, 44, 45
Ben Eliezer, Israel, 65
Ben Gershom, Rabbi Levi (Ralbag or Gersonides), 55
Ben Gurion, David, 75
Ben Isaac, Solomon (Rashi), 48
Ben Israel, Menasseh, 64
Ben Maimon, Moses (Rambam or Maimonides), 51, 98, 99
Ben Yehiel Asher, the Rosh, 55
Benjamin, Judah P., 69
Benjamin of Tudela, 51
Bernadette, 69
Bernard, 49
Bhai Nand Lal, 64
Bhakti, 38, 43, 54, 119, 120, 126
Bhattarahas, 49, 50
Bhudevi, 122
Bhuvaneshwari, 122
Bible, Christian, 102
Bin Laden, Osama, 80
Black Baptists, 71
Black Death, 55
Black Muslim movement, 77, 78
Blavatsky, H. P., 71
Blood sacrifice, 95
Blue Mosque, 58, 111
Blum, Léon, 75
Bodh Gaya, 25
Bodhidharma, 127
Bodhisattvas, 126, 127, 142
Boniface, 44
Boniface VIII, Pope, 55
Book of Common Prayer, 60, 64
Book of the Dead, 82
Book of Kells, 45
Book of Mormon, 70
Booth, William, 71
Born Again movement, 77
Boxer Rebellion, 71
Brahma, 32, 120
Brahman, 118, 119, 123
Brahmins (priests), 38
Brahmo Samaj, 68
Bray, Thomas, 64
Breatharians, 152
Brennus, 90
Bruno, 48
Bruno, Giordano, 63
Bubastis, 83
Buddha, the, 25, 36, 38, 117, 120, 124, 127
Buddhism: essence of beliefs, 125; festivals and holy days, 127; Mahayana, 126; origins, 25, 38; sacred writings, 125; Theravada, 126; Tibetan Buddhism, 127; Zen, 127

Cabot, John, 57
Caesar, Julius, 39, 89
Cairo, 47
Caishen, 143
Calvin, John, and Calvinism, 60, 61, 108
Cambridge Yiddish Codex, 56
Canaan, 34
Candomblé, 152
Canossa, 49
Canupa Wakan, 94
Cao Dai, 153
Cargo Cult, 153
Carmelite Order, 51
Carter, Jimmy, 77
Carthage, 38
Carthusian Order, 48
Cartoons of Muhammad, 80
Casimir the Great, 56
Cassiodorus, 45
Caste system, 123
Catfish, 146
Catholic Emancipation in Britain, 68
Celestial Masters, 48
Celtic religions, 90
Chalcedon, 43, 103
Chandaka, 25

Chandra Sen, Keshab, 69
Chandragupta, 39
Charismatic movement, 77
Charismatic Renewal, 109
Charlemagne, Emperor, 47
Chauhan, Janjit Singh, 80
Chavín culture, 36
Chenghuang, 143
Chinese religions: ancestor worship, 136; Confucius and religion, 138; Daoism, 140; gods, 142; origins, 27, 34
Chinmaya Mission, 72
Chinmayananda, Swami, 72
Chisti, Muin al-Din Muhammad, 51
Chitrabhanu, 72
Chmielnitsky, Boris, 63
Ch'oe Cheu, 69
Chola Empire, 48
Cholula, 56
Chondo, 69
Chondogyo, 72
Chou dynasty, 36
Creation mythologies, 31
Christ, Jesus, 26, 39, 40, 41, 102, 103, 110, 117
Christ (Scientist), Church of, 71
Christianity: Anglican communion, 107; Baptist church, 109; Eastern Orthodoxy, 107; essence of beliefs, 103; festivals, 105; Lutheranism, 108; Methodism, 109; origins, 26, 41; Pentecostalism, 109; Presbyterian churches, 108; Roman Catholicism, 106; scriptures, 102; worship, 104;
Christology, 41
Chrysostom, John, 43
Chumash, 59
Churning of the Waters, 32
Chusius, 50, 51
Civil Rights movement, 78
Clay, Cassius, 77
Clement V, Pope, 53, 55
Clement VII, Pope, 57
Clermont, 48
Clovis, King, 44, 45
Coke, Thomas, 109
Columba, 44
Columbus, Christopher, 57, 59, 94
Communion, Holy, 104
Communism, 73
Concordat, Napoleonic, 68
Confucian Classics, 138
Confucius (Kong Fuzi) and Confucianism, 27, 36, 38, 42, 44, 79, 136, 138, 139, 140, 141
Congregationalism, 65, 108
Conrad of Masovi, Duke, 49
Constance, 56, 57
Constantine I, Emperor, 41, 43
Constantinople, 44, 53, 58, 59
Consubstantiation, 61
Copan, 43, 45, 47
Copatra, Queen, 37
Cortés, Hernán, 60
Coventry Cathedral, 77
Cow slaughter dispute (Sikh), 71, 133
Cranmer, Thomas, 107
Creationism, 73, 102
Creation Museum, 80
Crete, 35, 86
Cronos, 32
Crusade, Children's, 52
Crusades, 48–53
Cuzco, 57, 95
Cyrus the Great, 36

Da Vinci Code, The, 80
Daibutsu, 45, 47
Dai Nipponshi, 144
dakhma, 97
Daksinamurti, 121
Dalai Lama, 61, 76, 80, 127

Dalip Singh, 70
Dalits, 80
Damascus blood libel, 68
Damasus, Pope, 43, 102
Danae, 86
Danka seido system, 62, 63
Dante Alighieri, 55
Dao and Daoism, 38, 136, 138, 140, 141, 144
Dao De Jing, 38, 140
Dao Sheng, 43
Darwin, Charles, 69, 71
Darshan, 130
Dasam Granth, 65, 132
David, King, 36 , 37, 99
Dayananda Sarasvati, 68
Dead Sea Scrolls, 75
Deguchi Nao, 72
Delhi, Sultanate of, 52, 54, 56, 62
Delphi, 38, 86, 87
Demeter, 87
Dervishes, 116
Devanampiya, 39
Devas, 32, 38, 122, 123
Dhanvantari, 32, 121
Dharma, 25, 38, 40, 118, 124
Dharmasala, 127
Dhikr, 115
Dhumavati, 122
Diagram of the Supreme Ultimate, 50
Diamond Way (Vajrayana), 127
Didyma, 38
Di Manes, 88
Digambara, 42, 128, 129, 130, 131
Diksha, 131
Dionysius Exiguus, 44
Dionysos, 87
Diocese, 45
Diocletian, 41
Disraeli, Benjamin, 69
Divine Faith, 62
Djenné, 115
Doctrine of the Mean, 139
Dodona, 38
Dogen, 52, 54, 127
Dolci, Giovanni de, 59
Dome of the Rock, 44
Dominic, 52
Dominican Order, 52, 57
Dong Zhongshu, 38
Dream Time, 93
Dreyfus, Captain Alfred, 69, 71, 72
Druids, 90
Druzes, 48, 115
Dukkha, 119, 125
Durga, 122
Dyal Das, 67

Ea, 32
Eckhart, Meister, 55
Eddy, Mary Baker, 71
Edict of Expulsion, 76
Edict of Nantes, 63, 64
Edirne, 58
Edwards, Jonathan, 65, 67
Egypt, ancient, religion of, 82
Eichmann, Adolf, 76
Eightfold Path, 126
Eightfold Worship, 130
Eight Immortals, 142
Eisai, 51, 127
Eisenstein, Ira, 101
El-Amara, 82
Eleusis, 87
Elijah Muhammad, 77, 78
Ema, 148
Embla, 32
Engishiki, 47, 144
England, Church of, 107
English civil wars, 63
Enil, 84
Enki, 84, 85
Enkidu, 85
Enlil, 85
Enoch, 110
Enryakuji temple, 61
Ephesus, 43
Epicurus, 87

Episcopal Church in Scotland, 107
Episcopal Church of the United States of America, 71, 80, 107
Epona, 90
Erasmus, Desiderius, 61, 62
Erdenedalai, 52
Erebus, 32
Eretz Israel, 69
Eridu, 84
Eris, 32
Erlitou culture, 34, 35
Eros, 32
Etemanaki, 37
Eucharist, 61, 104, 108
Eudocia, 43
Europa, 86
European Jain Association, 76
Evangelism, 77, 79, 108

Falun Gong, 80
Falwell, Jerry, 77, 80
Family Rights, Ottoman Law of, 72
Farid, 132
Fatehpur Sikri, 60
Fatima, 114
Fatimid dynasty, 47, 48
Faunus, 88
Feng Shui, 139
Finney, Charles, 68
Fire temple, 97
First Man, 96
Five Beloved Ones, 66
Five Elements, 50, 139, 141
Five Great Vows, Jain, 131
Five "K"s, 66
Five Northern Masters, 50
Five Pecks of Rice, Way of, 40
Five Pillars of Islam, 111
Five Precepts of Buddhism, 125, 126
Floating Bridge of Heaven, 32
Flood, Great, 35
Flora, 88
Florence, 57
Fountains Abbey, 61
Four Noble Truths, 125
Fox, George, 63, 64, 109
Francis of Assisi, 52, 61
Franciscan Order, 52, 55, 57
Frankel, Zecharias, 101
Frederick II, Emperor, 49, 52, 53
Frelinghuysen, Theodore, 65
French Revolution, 67
Frey/Freyr, 91
Freyja, 91
Frigg, 91
Fujiwara, 60
Fujiyama, 146
Fundamentalism, Christian, 77
Fushimi shrine, 151
Futsu nushi, 146
Fuxi, 42, 142

Gabriel, 112
Galileo Galilei, 63
Gama, Vasco da, 57, 59
Gandhi, Indira, 79
Gandhi, Mohandas Karamchand, 73, 74
Ganesha, 43, 121
Ganga, 121, 122
Ganges, River, 62, 80, 121, 133
Gaozong, 141
Garuda, 121
Gathas, 96
Gay adoption, 80
Gayomart, 32
Geb, 31
Ge Hong, 41, 141
Geiger, Abraham, 101
Gelugpa school, 54
General Baptists, 63
Genghis Khan, 54
German Faith Movement, 75
Germanic and Norse Gods, 91
Ghaiba, 47
Gilgamesh, 35, 84
Gitagovinda, 49
Glasnost, 77

Gobind Singh, Guru, 27, 62, 64, 66, 67, 134, 135
Golden Dawn, Hermetic Order of the, 154
Golden Mosque, Samarra, 80
Golden Pavilion of Kinkakuji, 56
Golden Temple, Amritsar, 60, 61, 62, 72, 79, 134, 135
Gongen, 147
Gospels, 102, 110
Goths, 43
Graham, Billy, 75, 79
Granada, 59
Grand Sanhedrin, 68
Grandison, Charles, 65
Great Awakening, 65, 67, 69, 109
Great Bible, 60
Great Schism, 49, 56, 57, 61, 108
Greece, ancient, religions of, 86
Gregorian calendar, 105
Gregorian chant, 44
Gregory I (the Great), Pope, 44, 45, 46
Gregory VII, Pope, 48, 49
Gregory IX, Pope, 52
Gregory XI, Pope, 57
Gui, 136
Gumi, 51
Gunabhada, 128
Gunapdesha movement, 78
Gunavratas, 131
Gunpowder Plot, 63
Guo Xiang, 41
Gupta Empire, 43
Gurdwara, 132, 134
Gurdwaras Act, 73, 74
Gurmat Prakas Bhag Sanskar reformist code, 72
Gurmukhi, 132
Gurpurb, 135
Gursikh, 133
Guru Granth Sahib, 62, 63, 66, 132, 134, 135
Gurus, Sikh, 27

Hachiman, 51, 146
Hadassah, 72
Hadith, 47, 50, 110, 111
Hadrian, Emperor, 40, 89
Hafez, Muhammad Shams ad-Din, 54, 56
Hafiz, 55
Hagia Sophia, 57, 58, 111
Hagiographa, 98
Haibutsu Kishaku ('Throw out the Buddhas'), 69
Haiden, 148
Haile Selassie, 73
Hajj, 80, 111, 113
Hajj Malik el-Shabazz, 78
Halevi, Judah, 48
Halevi ibn Nagrella, Samuel, 48
Halloween, 91
Hammurabi, King, 34, 35
Hanbleceya, 94
Handel, George Frideric, 67
Han dynasty, 139
Hanlin Academy, 45
Hanuman, 121
Haran, 24
Harappa, 35
Hare Krishna movement, 78
Hargobind, Guru, 27
Haribhadra, 44
Harimandir gurdwara, *see* Amritsar
Har Krishnan, Guru, 27
Har Rai, Guru, 27
Hasmoneans, 37, 39
Hassan, 115
Hassan al-Banna, 72
Hatam Sopher, 68
Hattin, Battle of, 49
Haumai, 133
Hayashi Razan, 62
Hayy ibn Yaqzan, 50
Headscarves, 80
Heavenly Masters, 40, 43, 48, 140
Hebrews, 24 , 34, 35, 36 , 36
Hemera, 32
Henry II, Emperor, 51
Henry IV, Emperor, 49
Henry VIII, King, 60, 61
Hera, 38
Heracles, 86
Heraclitus, 87
Hercules, 90
Hermetic Order of the Golden Dawn, 154
Herod the Great, 37
Herzl, Theodor, 59
Heschel, Abraham Joshua, 75
He Yan, 41
Hidetada, 62
Hideyoshi Toyotomi, 61, 62

Hillel, 39
Hinayana, 126
Hinduism: caste system, 123; essence of belief, 119; festivals, 123; Hindu gods, 120; origins, 38; sacred writing, 118; worship, 123
Hindu Marriage Act, 76
Hindu nationalism, 78
Hindu Renaissance, 70, 71
Hindutva movement, 78
Hirata Atsutane, 66
Hirohito, Emperor, 78
Hirsch, Baron de, 71
Hirschel, Solomon, 68
Hirvijaya Suir, 61
Hittites, 35
Hollywood, 72
Holocaust, 74, 75, 80
Holy Spirit Association for the Unification of World Christianity, 76
Holy Trinity, 103
Homer, 86
Homosexuality, 80, 107
Honden, 148
Honen, 51, 54
Hopi, 94
Horus, 83
Horyuji temple, 44
Hospitallers, 49
Huacas, 33, 95
Hua Hu Jin, 43
Huangdi, 140, 142
Hubbard, L. Ron, 76
Huexotzingo, 56
Huguenots, 64
Hukum Nama, 69, 134
Humanae Vitae, 76
Humayan's tomb, 60
Hun, 136
Hunkapi, 94
Huss, Jan, 56, 57, 61
Hussein, Saddam, 80

Ibn Rushd, 50, 51, 54, 116
Ibn Sina, Abu Ali Husayn (Avicenna), 50
Ibn Taymiyah, Taqi al-Din, 54
Ibn Tufayl, Abu Bakr (Abubacer), 50, 51
Icons and iconoclasm, 44, 46, 107
Iliad, 86
Imams, 112, 114
Imbolc, 91
Immaculate Conception, 69
Immortality in Daoism, 141
Imperial Rescript on Education, 69
Inanna, 84
Inari, 146
Incas, 48, 52, 57, 95
Indian Mutiny, 70
Indulgences, 61
Inipi, 94
Injil, 110
Inquisition, 52, 57, 59, 68
International Bible Students Association (Jehovah's Witnesses), 71
Inuit, 33, 94
Io, 93
Iraq, 80
Ireland, Church of, 107
Irenaeus, 40
Irene, Empress, 46
Irgun Zvi Leumi, 74
Isaac, 35, 102
Isamil I, 60
Ise Jingu, 145, 148
Isfahan, 97
Isis, 82
ISKCON, 76, 79
Islam: essence of belief, 111; festivals, 113; origins, 26, 45; scriptures, 110; sects, 114; sufism, 115; worship, 112
Ismailis, 45, 114
Isnati Awicaliwanpi, 94
Israel, 74, 75
Istanbul, 58
Ithna Ashariyya, 115
Ito Jinsai, 64
Ixipitla, 95
Izanagi, 32, 145
Izanami, 32, 145

Jacob, 24, 35, 102
Jade Emperor, 142
Jahan, Shah, 63
Jain Declaration on Nature, 79
Jainism: ascetics and lay Jains, 131; essence of beliefs, 129; festivals, 130; origins, 27, 38; scriptures, 128; worship, 130
Jansenism, 64

Japanese religions: New Religions, 150; origins, 42; Shinto, 144; Shinto literature, 144; Shinto mythology and deities, 145; shrines and temples, 147; worship and festivals, 149
Jatis, 123
Jayadeva, 49
Jayavarman VII, King, 52
Jefferson Bible, 68
Jehovah's Witnesses, 71
Jerusalem, 36 , 37, 40
Jesuits, 60, 67
Jesus, *see* Christ
Jewish Diaspora, 41
Jewish revolts, 40
Ji, 140
Jibril, 112
Jihad, 114
Jiin hatto (Ordinances for the temples), 64
Jin dynasty, 41, 43
Jinas, 27, 130, 131
Jinesvara Suri, 50
Jinguji, 146, 148
Jinja, 147
Jinja Honcho, 149
Jinja-kyoku (Shrine Offices), 72
Jinno Shotoki, 55, 144
Jisha Bugyo (Supervision Office of Temples and Shrines), 63
Jivan-mukta, 133
Jizya, 45, 64, 66
Jnana, 119
Joan of Arc, 56, 59
Jodo Shinsu (True Pure Land), 54
Jodo shu (Pure Land), 54
John the Baptist, 53
John Paul II, Pope, 79, 80
Johkang, 44, 76
Joshua, 24
Josiah, 36
Judah, 36
Judaism: essence of beliefs, 99; festivals and holy days, 99; modern Jewish beliefs, 101; nonorthodox strands in scriptures, 98; Sephardic and Ashkenazi Judaism, 101
Judas, 80
Julian the Apostate, 43
Julian of Norwich, 56
Jupiter, 88
Justinian I, Emperor, 44, 46, 57
Justin the Martyr, 40
Just War, 73

Ka'aba, 24, 26, 113
Kabbalah, 59, 154
Kabir, 59, 132
Kachina, 94
Kagutsuchi, 32, 146
Kagyu school, 54
Kaifeng, 55
Kaiser Wilhelm Memorial Church, 77
Kakazi Muneika, 146
Kali, 122
Kaliyuga, 120
Kalpa Sutra, 39, 128
Kama, 118
Kami, 42, 46, 145, 148
Kanishka, 124
Kanshi Ram, 80
Kaplan, Mordechai, 101
Karbala, 44, 45, 114
Karma, 38, 119, 124, 125, 129
Kartikaya, 121
Kashima god, 146
Kasyapa, 127
Kegon, 44
Kemal, Mustafa, "Ataturk," 73
Kennedy, John F., 76
Ketuvim, 40, 98
Kevalin, 129
Khalistan, 77, 80
Khalsa, 64, 66, 71, 135
Khmer, 47
Khomeini, Ayatollah, 77, 78, 79
Kimbanguism, 154
Kim Il Sung, cult of, 79
King, Martin Luther, 76
King James Version Bible, 63
Kingu, 32
Kino, 68
Kish, 34
Kishar, 32
Knossos, 86
Knox, John, 60, 108
Kohugaku (Japanese Studies) movement, 66
Kojiki, 44, 46, 144
Kong Fuzi, *see* Confucius

Konkokyo, 150
Konrad III, Emperor, 49
Kosovo, Battle of, 56, 58
Koutoubia, 48
Krishna, 35, 117, 120, 123
Krishna Consciousness, International Society for, 78
Kronos, 86
Kuan Ti, 143
Kuan Yin, 143
Kukai, 47
Kumarapala, 52
Kunado no kami, 146
Kundakunda, 128
Kurma, 32, 120
Kurozumikyo, 68, 150
Kurozumi Munetada, 68
Kyanzittha, 48

Ladnun, 76
Lagash, 34
Lahmu, 32
Lakota, 94
Lakshmi, 32, 121, 122
Lam Rim, 127
Langar, 133
Laozi, 24, 38, 40, 42, 140
Lares, 88
Larsa, 84
Las Navas de Tolosa, Battle of, 52
Last Supper, 104
Lateran Councils, 51, 52, 104
Lateran Treaty, 73
Latter-Day Saints, Church of Jesus Christ of, 70
Laubach, Frank, 76
Lehna, 60
Lei Gong, 143
Leo III, Pope, 46
Lewis, Curtis Lee, 77
Li, 50, 138, 139
Lieze, 140
Lijing, 136
Limbo, 80
Lingbao, 41
Liu Shaoqi, 76
Liverpool, 7
Livingstone, David, 69
Li Xuan, 50
Lollards, 56
Lombard, Peter, 49, 104
London Missionary Society, 67
Lotus Sutra, 52, 126
Louis VII, King, 49
Louis IX, King, 52, 53
Louis XIV, King, 64
Lourdes, 69
Loyola, Ignatius, 60
Lucan, 90
Luther, Martin, 60, 61, 108
Lutheran Council in the United States of America, 76, 108
Lutheran World Federation, 75, 108
Lutherism, 108
Lu Xiujing, 43

Ma'at, 82
Machu Picchu, 52
Madhra, 52, 53
Maghada, 36
Mahabarata, 35, 38, 118, 120, 121
Mahabodhi Temple, 75
Mahadevi, 122
Mahapranjna, 72
Mahavarata, 131
Mahavira, 27, 36, 38, 128
Mahayana, 40, 54, 124, 126
Mahdi movement, 59, 71
Maimonides, Moses ben, 51, 98, 99
Malacca, 58, 59
Malcolm X, 78
Malta, 49
Mandate of Heaven, 36
Mandora, Mount, 32
Mani, 41
Manichaeism, 41
Manu, 118
Manzikert, Battle of, 48, 49
Mao Shan Shang-ch'ing, 41, 43
Mao Zedong, 75
Mara, 25
Marae, 93
Marathas, 66, 67
March for Jesus, 79
Marduk, 32, 34, 37, 84, 85
Margas, 119
Martin V, Pope, 57
Marx, Karl, 73
Masands, 66
Mashad al-Husayn, 114

Masjid al-Aqsa mosque, 50
Mass, 46, 80, 104
Masyad, 115
Matangi, 122
Mathura, 39
Matsuri, 149
Matsurigoto, 42
Matsya, 120
Mauryan Empire, 39
Mayan Empire, 43, 44, 47, 52, 95, 119
Mayflower, 63, 108
Mayon, 120
Mecca, 24, 45, 110, 111, 112, 113, 114
Medina, 45, 110
Megiddo, 36
Mehmet II, 59
Meiji Era, 46, 55, 66, 69, 71, 73, 148
Melanesia, 93
Menander, 38
Mencius, 39, 139
Mendelssohn, Moses, 67, 101
Mengzi, 39, 139
Mercury, 90
Meru, Mount, 32
Methodist Church, 75
Methodist Episcopal Church, 67
Methodists, 65, 109
Michael II Paleologus, Emperor, 80
Midgard, 32, 91
Midzuchi, 146
Miko, 42
Milton, John, 64
Minamoto Yorimoto, 51, 63
Mingdi, 40
Minoans, 35, 86
Minos, 86
Mirza Ghulam Ahmad Qadiyani, 71
Mirza Husayan 'Ali Nuri, 117
Mishna, 40, 43, 98
Misogi, 149
Mitama, 145
Mithras, 39, 41, 88, 89
Mogul Empire, 58, 60, 62, 64, 67
Mohendjo-Daro, 35
Moksha, 38, 40, 118, 119, 129
Moksha marg, 129
Molcho, Solomon, 60
Möngke, Khan, 54
Mongol Empire, 52, 54
Monophysites, 41
Monte Cassino, 45
Montefiore, Moses, 68
Monty Python's Life of Brian, 77
Moody, Dwight Lyman, 69
Moon, Sun Myung, 76
Moonies, 76
Mootokyo Shinto, 72
Moral Majority, 77, 80
Mormons, 68, 70, 78
Moroni, 70
Moses, 24, 34, 37, 98, 102
Moses de Leon, 53
Moses Sopher, 68
Mozi, 139
Mu'awiyyah ibn Abi-Sufayan, 45
Muezzin, 112
Muhammad, 24, 44, 45, 110, 112, 114, 117
Muhammad Abduh, 71
Muhammad Ali, 77
Muhammad of Ghor, 51
Mukti, 133
Müller, Max, 68
Mul Mantra, 132
Mummu, 32
Munich Olympic Games, 76
Muqanna, 114
Mutazilites, 114

Nabi, 110
Nabonidus, 37
Nadir Shah, 67
Nagasaki, 61, 63, 66, 75
Nagi Gluhapi, 94
Nakayama Mik, 68
Nalanda, 43, 51
Namazu, 146
Namdharis (or Kookas), 68, 70
Nanak, Guru, 27, 57, 60, 70, 132, 135
Nanakshahi, 135
Nanna, 84
Nantes, Edict of, 63, 64
Napoleon, 68
Nara, 44, 46
Narak, 59
Narankiri movement, 70
Narasingha, 120
Nasrids, 52
Nataraja, 40, 121

Nation of Islam, 77, 78
Nauvoo, 70
Navjote, 97
Nayanars, 49
Nazca civilization, 39
Nazis, 74, 75
Nebuchadnezzar, King, 34, 85
Nehemiah, 37
Nemesis, 32
Neo-Confucianism, 47, 48, 50
Neoplatonism, 41, 89, 116
Nepthys, 82
Neptune, 39
Nero, Emperor, 40
Nestorians, 47, 48, 54
Nevi'im, 98
New American Standard Bible, 76
New Testament, 102
Newton, Sir Isaac, 64
Ngunzism, 154
Nicaea, 43, 45, 46
Nichiren, 52, 54
Niflheim, 32
Nihongi/Nihonshoki, 46, 144, 146
Nimbarka school, 56
Nineveh, 85
Ninigi, 46
Ninigi-no-mikoto, 145
Ninurta, 84
Nippur, 84
Nirvana, 125, 126
Nirvana Sutra, 126
Njord, 91
Noah, 35
Nobel Peace Prize, 75, 109
Noble Eightfold Path, 125
Nobunaga Oda, 62
Normans, 48
Norns, 91
North American belief systems, 94
Northern Baptist Convention, 72
Northern Ireland, 76
No Ruz, 97
Norwich, 51, 55
Nôtre Dame, 105
Nu Kua, 143
Numitor, 88
Nu Wa, 32
Nyorai-kyo, 68
Nyx, 32

Obaku Zen, 127
Odin, 32, 91
Odyssey, 86
Office of Divine Affairs, 69
Ogmios, 90
Ogun, 32
Ogyu Sorai, 64
Oho-na-mochi, 145
Olcott, Henry Steel, 71
Old Testament, 102
Olmec civilization, 36, 40
Olympia, 38
Olympus, 32, 86
Ometeotl, 95
On the Origin of Species, 69
Opus Dei, 73, 80
Oracle bone, 35, 136
Order of the Solar Temple, 155
Original Sin, 103
Orléans, 59
Orthodox Judaism, 99
Osiris, 82, 88
Ottomans, 58, 59, 73
Oxford Movement, 68
Oya-ko, 145
Ozman, Agnes N., 72

Padres, 73
Paekche, 44
Paek Ijong, 55
Paestum, 39
Pagan (Burma), 45, 48, 53, 54
Pale of Settlement, 68
Palestine Liberation, Organization, 76
Pali, 53
Palm Sunday, 41
Pangat, 133
Pan Gu, 32
Papa, 32
Paradise Lost, 64
Parasparopagrahojivanam, 129
Parasurama, 120
Parsis, 33, 45, 66
Parthenon, 36
Parvati, 121, 122
Pasiphae, 86
Patna, 39
Patriarchates, 107
Patrick, 43
Paul, 40, 41, 102
Peloponnesian Wars, 87

Penn, William, 64
Pentateuch, 24, 37, 98
Pentecostalism, 109
Peres, Shimon, 79
Perestroika, 77
Perfection of Wisdom suttas, 126
Perfect Life Kyodan, 151
Persephone, 87
Perseus, 86
Peru, 36
Peter, 40, 106
Peter the Great, 65
Petrel, 94
Philadelphia Baptist Association, 64
Philae, 37
Philip IV, King, 55
Philip the Fair, 53
Philippines, 40
Phillip II, King, 87
Phocas, 46
Pietism, 64
Pilgrim Fathers, 63, 109
Pisa, 57
Pius VII, Pope, 68
Plato, 37, 87
Plotinus, 40, 89
Plymouth Brethren, 68
Poland, 47
Polo, Marco, 115
Polynesia, 93
Polyphemus, 86
Pompeii, 88
Pontifex Maximus, 39
Port-Royal, 64
Portuguese, 66
Poseidon, 39, 86
Positive Christianity, 75
Potala Palace, Lhasa, 79
Prabandham, 47
Prague, 57
Pragya, 125
Praise of Folly, 61
Prambanan, 47
Predestination, 108
Presbyterian Churches, General Assembly of, 67
Presbyterians, 65, 67, 108
Priapus, 88
Promethus, 32
Promised Land, 99
Psammetichus I, King, 37
Ptolemaic dynasty, 37, 39
Puja, 38, 123
Puranas, 38, 118
Pure Land (Jodo-shu), 51, 127
Puritans, 108
Purushartha, 118
Purvas, 128
Pyramids, 33

Qadiryyas, 115, 116
Qajars, 67
Qanun, 50
Qarmatians, 114
Qi, 50, 139, 140
Qibla, 112
Quakers, 75, 109
Quaker World Council of Friends, 72
Quanzhen Daoist reform movement, 49, 52
Quetzalcoatl, 95
Qufu, 59
Qur'an, 24, 44, 45, 50, 54, 102, 110, 111, 112, 114, 115
Qutub Minar, Delhi, 53

Rabbinical Period, 52
Rabindranath Tagore, 72
Rachamalla, 47
Ragis, 134
Ragnarok, 91
Rahit Maryada, 76, 134
Rahits, 67
Raikes, Robert, 67
Rajachandra, Shrimad, 71
Rakah, 112
Ram, Kanshi, 80
Rama, 35, 120, 121
Ramakrishna, 68
Ramanuja, 48, 119
Ramanujacharya, 119
Ramayana, 38, 118, 120, 121, 122
Ramcaritamanasa, 63
Ram Mohan Roy, 68
Ramses II, Pharaoh, 33, 34, 35
Ram Singh, 68
Rangi, 32
Ranjit Singh, 67, 68, 70
Rashid Rida, 71

Rastafari, 73, 155
Rasuls, 110
Ratri, 122
Ratzinger, Joseph, 80
Rav, 40
Ravana, 121
Ravidas, 132
Razan Hayashi, 60
Re, 31, 82–3
Reformation, 62, 102, 108
Reform Society, 68
Reims, 56
Reiyukai Kodan, 73, 150
Remus, 88
Ren, 138
Rénouveau Charismatique, 77
Reubeni, David, 60
Revivalism, 69
Reza Pahlavi, Shah Muhammad, 78
Rhazes, 47
Rhea, 86, 88
Rhodes, 49
Richard I, King, 49, 51
Rifais, 116
Rightly Conducted Caliphs, 44
Rig Veda, 32, 123
Rindfleisch, 55
Rinzai Zen Buddhism, 51, 55, 127
Rio de Janeiro, 75
Rishi, 118
Rissho Koseikai, 75
Robespierre, Maximilien, 67
Robinson, Vicky Imogene "Gene," 80
Rokkokushi, 144
Rome, ancient, religions of, 88
Romulus, 88
Rosmerta, 90
Rothschild, Lionel, 69, 74
Rushdie, Salman, 79
Russell, Charles Taze, 71
Ryoan-ji temple, 59
Ryobu Shinto, 46

Sabah State Mosque, 116
Sacraments, Christian, 104
Sacred Songs and Solos, 69
Sadharan Brahmo Samaj, 71
Safavid dynasty, 58, 67
Sagrada Família, 78
Saicho, 47
Sakas, 39
Sakoku, 63
Sakya school, 54
Saladin, 49, 51
Salafiya, 71
Salem witchcraft trials, 64
Salt Lake City, 68, 70
Salvation Army, 71
Samadhi, 125
Samarra, 80
Samhain, 91
Samsara, 38, 119, 129
Sanchi, 40
Sangat, 133, 134
Sangha, 25, 126
Sankey, Ira David, 69
Sant tradition, 56
Sanusiya, 68
Saoshyant, 96
Saqqara, 33, 35
Saraswati, 122
Sargon I, King, 35
Satan, 25
Satanic Verses, The, 79
Satanism, 156
Saudi Arabia, 73, 75
Saul, 35
Savonarola, Girolamo, 59
Sawmj, 113
Sayyid 'Ali Muhammad, 117
Sayyid Qutb, 76
Schechter, Solomon, 101
Schism, Great, *see* Great Schism
Scholastics, 45, 50
Schori, Katherine Jefferts, 80
Schweitzer, Albert, 72
Scientists, Christian, 71
Scientology, Church of, 76, 80, 156
Scofield Reference Bible, 72
Scopes, John T., 73
Scotland, Church of, 107
Scythians, 39
Sea Peoples, 34
Sea Woman, 94
Sekai Kyuseikyo, 73, 151
Self-Empowerment Academy (Breatharians), 152
Sengensama, 146
Sephardim, 101

Seth, 110
Seven Sages of the Bamboo Grove, 41
Sex abuse by priests, 80
Shabbetai Zevi, 64
Shahada, 111
Shaiva-Siddhanta, 49
Shakti, 122
Shamanism, 33, 92, 94
Shamash, 34, 85
Shammai, 39
Shang Di, 35, 137, 138
Shang dynasty, 34, 35, 136, 137
Shankaracharya, 119
Shari'ah, 54, 78, 110, 112, 115
She, 136
Shen, 136
Shennung, 142
Shi'a Islam, 45, 114, 115
Shi'ite-Ismailis, 47
Shila, 125
Shimenawa, 148
Shin, 139
Shingon, 47
Shinran-shonin, 52, 54
Shintai, 145, 145, 149
Shinto, 144–149
Shiva, 38, 40, 121, 120, 121, 123
Shoah, 74, 75
Shoghi Effendi, 117
Shoku Nihongi, 45, 144
Shomu, Emperor, 46
Shotoku, 44
Shotoku Taishi, Prince Regent, 46
Shravanbelagola, 47
Shrutis, 118
Shu, 31
Shugendo, 147
Shukyo-kyoku (Religion Offices), 72
Shun, 137
Shutruk-Nahhunte, 34
Shvetambaras, 42, 44, 50, 128, 129, 130, 131
Siddhartha, Gautama (the Buddha), 25, 36, 38, 117, 120, 124, 127
Sikh Ghadr movement, 72
Sikhism: essence of beliefs, 133; festivals, 135; origins, 27, 57; scriptures, 132; Sikh community, 135; worship, 134
Siksavratam, 131
Silence, Tower of, 97
Silent Sermon, 127
Silvanus, 88
Simon of Trent, 59
Sin, the moon god, 37
Sinai, 24, 99
Singh Sabha, 70, 71
Singhvi, L. M., 79
Sioux, 94
Sistine Chapel, 59, 60
Sita, 121, 122
Skandhas, 125
Slavery, 68, 71, 109
Smith, Joseph, 70
Smritis, 118
Society for Promoting Christian Knowledge (SPCK), 64
Socrates, 37, 87
Sol Invictus, 41, 89
Solomon, King, 36, 37
Somadeva, 47
Sonam Gyatso, 61
Soto Zen Buddhism, 52, 54, 127
Spanish Armada, 61
Spener, Jakob, 64
Spenta Mainyu, 96
Spiritualism, 156
Sravaka, 124
Sri Chand, 62
Srila Prabhupada, 78
Srivijaya, 47
Sthanakvasi, 56, 128, 130
Stalin, Joseph, 75
Stoicism, 87
Stonehenge, 90
Stravakayana, 126
Sufism, 48, 115, 116
Sugi trees, 148
Sui Jen, 143
Sukhothai, 54
Sukuna-bikona, 145
Sulis Minerva, 88
Sultan Ahmed Mosque, 58

Sumeria, 84
Sunday school, 67
Sung dynasty, 47
Sunna, 111
Sunni Islam, 114
Suppiluliumas II, King, 84
Supreme Being, Cult of the (French Revolution), 67
Sura Academy, 40
Suryavarman II, King, 51
Susa-no-wo, 32, 145
Svetambara, 65
Swedenborg, Emanuel, 65
Szold, Henrietta, 72

Tagi al-Din Ibn, 53
Tahafut al-Tahafut, 50
Tahara (purification), 112
Taiji, 50
Taika Reforms, 46
Taiping Rebellion, 69
Taiwu, Emperor, 43
Taj Mahal, 63
Takhats, 134
Taliban, 78, 79, 80
Talmud, 38, 44, 98
Tanakh, 98
Tangaroa, 32, 93
Tanit, 38
Tannenberg, Battle of, 56
Tantric Hinduism, 44
Tantrism, 127
Tao Qian, 43
Tapa Wankaye, 94
Tapu, 93
Taranapanthi, 130
Taranga, 52
Tartarus, 86
Tattvarthasutra, 43, 128
Tawrat, 110
Taylor, Nathaniel, 65
Taymiyah, 53
Tefnut, 31
Tegh Bahadur, Guru, 64, 67, 132, 135
Televangelism, 77, 79, 80
Temmangu, 146
Templars, 49, 55
Temple of Heaven, 56
Ten Commandments, 103
Tendai, 47
Tennant, Jr, William, 65
Tenochtitlan, 55, 59
Tenrikyo, 68, 150
Tensho Kotai Jingukyo, 151
Teotihuacan, 40
Terapanthi, 65, 75, 128, 130, 131
Terauke seido, 64
Teresa, Mother, 76
Test Act, 64
Teton, 94
Teutates, 90
Teutonic Knights, 49, 56
Thanos, 32
Thebes, 33
Theophilus, Emperor, 46
Theosophical Society, 71
Theravada, 38, 40, 54, 57, 124, 126, 127
Thirteen Principles of Judaism, 98
Thirty Years War, 63
Thor, 91
Thoth, 83
Three Caverns (Daoist), 43
Three Jewels of Buddhism, 46, 125
Three Jewels of Jainism, 43, 128
Three-in-One Religion, 61
Tiahuanaco, 95
Tiamat, 32
Tian, 36, 137, 138, 139, 142
Tian I Yuan, 142
Tian Ming, 138
Tianshi, 140
Tian Tsun, 142
Tibetan Buddhism, 127
Tijaniya, 115
Tikal, 95
Timur, 56
Tirthankaras, 27, 38, 130, 131
Ti-Tsang Wang, 143
Titus, Emperor, 40
Tlatelolco, 55, 56
Todai-ji, 45, 46, 47
Tokugawa Ieyasu, 63
Toledo, 44, 45
Toleration Act, 64
Toltec Empire, 48, 49, 52, 95
Tongues, speaking in, 72, 109
Topeka, 109

Torah, 24, 37, 98, 99, 100, 101, 102, 110
Torii, 148
Torquemada, Tomás de, 57, 59
Toshogu shrine, 62
Toyotomi Hideyoshi, 63
Transubstantiation, 61, 104, 108
Trent, 57, 60, 102, 104
Trimurti, 120
Trinity, Holy, 103
Tripitaka, 43, 124, 125, 126, 141
True Pure Land (Jodo-shinshu), 52
Tsong-kha-pa, 56
Tsukiyomi, 145
Tu Kuang-t'ing, 47
Tula, 49
Tulsi, 75
Tulsidas, 63
Tung Yueh Ta Ti, 142
Tutankhamun, Pharaoh, 33, 35
T'u-ti, 143
Twelve-Limbed Basket, The, 128
Tzolkin, 95

Udasi, 62
Udgard, 91
Udwada, 97
Uganda, 77
Uganda Controversy, 72
Ujigami, 42
Uke mochi, 146
Umar, 45
Umar Mosque, 44
Umayyad dynasty, 45
Umma, 34
Unification of World Christianity, Holy Spirit Association for the, 76
United Church of Canada, 76
United Methodist Church, 76
United Methodist Conference, 72
Upanishads, 36, 118, 119
Upashraya, 131
Ur, 33, 34, 35, 84
Urania, 157
Uranus, 86
Urban II, Pope, 48, 49
Urban V, Pope, 57
Uruk, 84
Usas, 122
Ussher, James, 33, 35, 64
Uthman, 45
Utu, 84

Vahanas, 122
Vairocana, 45
Vajrayana, 124, 127
Valabhi, 39, 42, 43, 128
Valdes, Peter, 51
Vamana, 120
Vanaraja, 45
Vanir deities, 91
Varaha, 120
Varnas, 38, 40, 123
Vars, 132
Vatican, 106
Vatican Councils: Vatican I, 71; Vatican II, 57, 76, 109
Ve, 32
Vedas, 34, 35, 38, 118
Venice, 49
Versailles, 73
Vesta, 88
Vijayanagar, 55, 56, 60
Vili, 32
Viracocha, 95
Vira-Shaivism, 51
Vishnu, 32, 38, 40, 120, 121, 123
Vishva Hindu Parishad, 72
Visigoths, 45
Visistadvaita-Vedanta school, 48
Vladimir, Prince of Kiev, 47
Vulgate, 102

Wahhabi sect, 54, 67, 73
Wakan Tanka, 94
Waldensians, 51
Waldo, Peter, 61
Wales, Church in, 107
Wali, 115
Wangdao, 139
Wang Fou, 43
Wang Pi, 41
Wang Yangming, 59, 62
Wang Zhe, 49
Way of Filial Piety, 44

Way of Heaven, 69, 139
Way of the Heavens, School of the, 72
Wepwawet, 82
Wesley, Charles, 65
Wesley, John, 65, 109
Whitby, Synod of, 44
Whitefield, George, 65, 67
Wicca, 157
Wilberforce, William, 68
Wine, Sherwin, 101
Wittenberg, 60, 61
Wiwanyag Wacipi, 94
Woden, 32, 91
Wojtyla, Karol, 76
Women priests, 79, 107
World Buddhist Sangha Council, 76
World Council of Churches, 75
World Parliament of Religions, 71
World Trade Center, 79, 80
World War I, 73
World War II, 75
Worms, 61
Wotan, 32, 91
Wudi, 38, 39
Wu Hsing, 141
Wycliffe, John, 56, 57, 61

Xavier, Francis, 60
Xia dynasty, 137
Xiangxiu, 41
Xiaodao, 44
Xing, 140
Xin Xue, 59
Xiuhtecuhtli, 95
Xiwang, 143
Xunzi, 39, 139

Yahweh, 31, 34
Yamato, 43, 46
Yamato-dake, 146
Yamazaki Ansai, 62
Yang and Yin, 32, 50, 139, 141
Yao, 137
Yasuhiro, Prime Minister Nakasone, 79
Yasukuni shrine, 150
Yazdegird III, 45
Yellow Hat order, 56
Yellow Turbans, 40
Yemen, 115
Yggdrasil, 91
Yi, 138
Yin, *see* Yang
Yitzhak Rabin, 79
Ymir, 32
Yochanan ben Zakkai, 40
Yogas, 119
Yomei-gaku, 62
York, 51
Yoruba, 92
Young, Brigham, 68, 70
Yu, 137
Yu Chao, 143
Yugas, 118
Yuzun-ambutsu, 49

Zabur, 110
Zaidis, 115
Zakah, 111
Zang Dao Lin, 42
Zarathustra, 96
Zen, 43, 54, 127
Zeno of Citium, 87
Zeus, 32, 36, 38, 86, 87
Zhenzong, Emperor 48
Zhongshu, 39
Zhongyong, 139
Zhou Dunyi, 48, 50
Zhou dynasty, 137
Zhuangzi, 38, 39, 140, 141
Zhu Xi, 50, 51
Ziggurats, 33, 34, 37, 84, 85
Zionism, 69, 72, 74
Zisi, 139
Zola, Emile, 69
Zoroaster and Zoroastrianism, 33, 35, 36, 37, 45, 96
Zuowang, 143
Zurich, 61
Zurvan, 32
Zwingli, Huldrych, 60, 61